Spiral of Shame

Dr. Covington —
Thanks for your help with
this project!

Jim m-Bet
Marcus Golden

Spiral of Shame

Confronting your Demons

Jeanne Peterson, Ph.D.
Marcie Goldman, Ph.D.

Humanics Publishing Group
Atlanta, GA

Humanics Trade Group Publications are an imprint of and pub-
lished by Humanics Publishing Group, a division of Humanics
Limited. Its trademark, consisting of the words "Humanics Trade
Group" and the portrayal of a Pegasus, is registered in U.S. Patent
and Trademark Office and in other countries.

Printed in the United States of America
Library of Congress Catalog Card Number: 99-0670598
ISBN: 0-89334-305-6

Humanics Limited
PO Box 7400
Atlanta, GA 30357

Table of Contents

Falling into the Spiral

Nancy's hand shook as she opened the door to her house. Her boss had been at it again, criticizing her work and destroying her credibility behind her back. She had felt her coworkers looking, staring at her, and then her friend Susan had told her what her boss had said.

Her thoughts went around what she'd heard, trying to untangle the mess she was in. As she walked into her bedroom, she had the sensation that she was falling into a space where she would just go round and round in anguished circles, unable to stop hating herself. As she climbed into her bedroom closet, she thought of this falling space as a spiral. She did not know how to escape once she was in it.

As she sat down on the closet floor, she hid herself behind the hanging clothes. I'll never come out of here, she thought. Hugging herself, she began rocking back and forth, trying to soothe away the loathing she felt for herself.

Learning to Escape
from the "Spiral of Shame"

Although it was originally used in a humorous way, the term "spiral of shame" accurately describes the overwhelming feelings of shame and guilt Nancy was experiencing. Because moderate shame and guilt are normal human emotions, you will probably feel shame and guilt at some point in your life.

However, when these emotions are excessive and over-whelming, they can become a very destructive force that can lead to depression, self-hate, self-destructive behavior, and an inability to give and receive love.

Purpose

The purpose of this book is to do three things:

1. Identify whether you have excessive shame and guilt;
2. Understand the origins of shame and guilt in your life; and most importantly,
3. Learn how to eliminate its effects on your mind and body.

Accordingly, the book is divided into three parts.

In part one, we present current definitions of shame and guilt, and provide activities to help you explore the role of these emotions in your life. Part two is spread across two chapters. The first of these chapters explores the ways in which our cultural environment can create shame and guilt. The second of the chapters in part two presents the ways in which we were taught to feel shame and guilt in the families in which we grew up. In part three, we present an active, holistic approach to healing from shame and guilt.

This approach involves healing the mind, the body, the emotions, and even our actions. Accordingly, there are exercises and activities to address each of these parts of us.

PART 1:

UNDERSTANDING SHAME AND GUILT

CHAPTER 1

AN INTRODUCTION
TO SHAME AND GUILT

Developing an Understanding
of Shame and Guilt

What are Shame and Guilt?

Shame and guilt are often thought of as being the same feeling, but there are several differences between these two emotions. Shame can be defined as the perception and feeling that you, as a human being, are defective and unworthy in some fundamental way, or that there is something wrong with you. When you make mistakes or feel vulnerable, you judge and criticize yourself as unworthy rather than seeing that making mistakes and feeling vulnerable are just part of being human. You may find yourself avoiding eye contact with others, hiding from others or withdrawing from those close to you. When you think in shaming ways, you criticize yourself harshly and you may even dislike or hate yourself. Some people call this process "beating yourself up." The shaming voice that you hear deep inside of you may tell you that you are unworthy to be loved or even to continue living.

In contrast to shame, guilt involves a focus on the unacceptable nature of your actions rather than on your being itself. For example, when a guilt-prone individual calls in sick to work because of bronchitis, he might think, "I should not have called in sick. Calling in sick is a bad thing to do. I let my coworkers down." In contrast, a shame-based individual might think, "I am a terrible person for calling in sick. I am unreliable and worthless." Thoughts about guilt involve a focus on what you have done, not who you are. When you experience guilt, you might try to correct some unacceptable action, or you might even try to cover up that action so that it is not discovered by others. People who feel guilty usually want to go back and change their actions.

For example, if you feel guilty because you answered irritably when your neighbor greeted you, you might think about the scenario over and over trying to determine how you should have responded. You might even make a point of saying "hello" and being very friendly to that neighbor the next chance that you get.

Feeling shame or guilt is not a pleasant experience, and so it is natural to avoid it as much as possible. There are many ways to avoid dealing with feelings of shame or guilt. You may avoid feeling shame by doing self-destructive things like using alcohol, drugs, food or indulging in other addictions to numb out the unpleasant feelings. Perhaps you avoid feeling and dealing with your shame by becoming extremely skilled at taking care of others and pleasing them, by being a "caretaker." As long as you are pleasing others, you are too busy for your feelings, and by doing "self-less" things, you are less likely to be criticized in a way that would trigger your feelings of shame. Workaholism is another way of maintaining such a busy schedule and such a distance from other people that you can hold shame feelings at bay.

Aside from trying to escape shame and guilt through these methods, you might also evade them by using defensive or even offensive tactics. If you find that you spend a lot of time defending yourself in front of other people, it's likely that you're really trying to fend off feelings of shame or guilt.

For example, imagine Inez, who spends a great deal of her time defending herself from feelings of guilt. At work she is known for having a terrible time receiving feedback from her superiors and even from coworkers. No matter how minor the feedback may be, she comes up with a reason to justify the way she does things. What is happening inside Inez is that she has a pro-found sense of guilt, and feels that nothing she does is good enough, and she feels the threat of a serious guilt episode whenever someone tries to give her feedback. Therefore, when a coworker comments on her work, she simply must convince that person that there is nothing wrong with her work. When others comment on her work, she feels it as an attack on her very being, and so she must defend herself.

In slight contrast, Michael, who suffers from excessive shame, operates under the old saying, "the best defense is a good offense." He spends a great deal of his energy pointing out the flaws and mistakes of others in a hopeless attempt to divert attention away from his own flaws. The added "benefit" of this particular method of running away from shame feelings is that criticizing others helps him maintain an attitude of superiority. Every day, a constant stream of negativity and biting criticism about others flows from his mouth.

Unfortunately, these methods of running from shame and guilt do not make them go away. In order to leave shame and guilt behind us we need to go through a healing process that involves looking within ourselves to the roots of our shame and guilt. We must understand that at some point in our past, seeds of shame or guilt were planted in us by someone or something in our environment. The people who were most important to us in our early years planted these seeds which now determine how we feel about who we are and all that we do. Those seeds grew into a critical inner voice that now comments on the everyday events of our adult lives.

For example, if you had a shaming parent who frequently told you "you are stupid," you probably started to believe that you actually are stupid. Now, whether that parent is present or not, you may still hear that voice inside your head telling you that you're stupid. Whenever something goes wrong, you may see your inferiority as the reason for it. In place of these shaming and blaming voices we must build a compassionate voice which accepts our human frailties, forgives us after we have made amends, and actually celebrates when we do the right thing.

Examples Of Shame And Guilt

The following examples may help further illustrate the different experiences of shame and guilt. Richard was working on a statistics project on the school computer, and found he was having some trouble getting the computer to perform the statistical analyses he needed. His head began to throb, and he felt like he couldn't breathe. He imagined that everyone in the room could tell that he was having trouble, and they probably all thought that he was an idiot. If only the floor could swallow him up right now, he thought. He stood up and walked quickly outside and desperately tried to find a place to be alone.

Once outside, he tried to calm himself down, and

noticed a voice in his head saying that he was the dumbest, most worthless human being on earth. He could hear his father's voice in his head saying that some people just don't have the brains to make it in college, and he felt sure that this computer difficulty was proof that he didn't have what it takes. Richard was experiencing a very intense shame episode.

As another example, let us consider Joan. She suffered from an acute episode of guilt after the following sequence of events. She was at work, and she was checking her voice mail. She received a very angry voice mail message from her boss, demanding to know why she hadn't responded to a voice mail message he said he had left two weeks before.

Joan knew that she had not received any message from him in the preceding two weeks, but it didn't matter. She instantly began to go over and over why she had not responded to the voice mail. She knew that her boss was angry with her, and she felt that she truly had done something wrong. Her heart began to pound, and she felt weak and shaky all over. Even though she left a voice mail message for her boss carefully explaining the situation, she still felt that somehow she had done something wrong, and she kept worrying over it for the rest of the day.

In this example, along with the intense guilt feelings

Joan experiences, there is guilt-related worrying, accompanying panicky feelings, and actions to correct the situation. Joan is focused on something that she thinks she did wrong, rather than on some defect within herself.

Shame and guilt can be elicited by very similar situations, except that shame usually follows a public exposure of one's weakness or failure. The eliciting situation alone does not seem to determine whether it will be shame, guilt, or both which follow. Each person's particular history, temperament, and thinking patterns act together along with particulars of the situation in determining whether that person will react with shame, guilt or both.

ACTIVITY 1:

UNDERSTANDING SHAME AND GUILT

For all activities in this book, you may use extra pages any time you need more space to write down your answers. Since you may want to go back and read it some time in the future, you might want to write your answers in a journal.

When you read through Richard's experience of shame, could you relate to his experience?

If so, how?

When you read through Joan's experience of
guilt, could you relate to it?

_____

In what ways?

_____

_____

_____

_____

_____

_____

_____

_____

How are shame and guilt different from each
other?

_____

_____

_____

How are shame and guilt alike?

_____

_____

_____

_____

Why Do We Experience
Shame and Guilt?

Although they can be painful emotions, especially if experienced in excess, shame and guilt are important in preserving societal rules and moral conduct. Sometimes we feel guilty for doing something "wrong." Because these feelings are not pleasant, we then strive to avoid guilt feeling by trying to do the "right" thing. Without some guilt or pangs of conscience, we would never be forced to examine our actions and follow ethical and moral guidelines of conduct.

For example, if you lived in a society without guilt, you could kill your own brother and never suffer feelings of guilt. Since you did not feel any guilt after killing your brother, there would be no trigger telling you that you have done something wrong. Similarly, we need some shame, because there are some situations in which feelings of shame are appropriate. These feelings of shame help us to follow the morally appropriate course of action.

Imagine a society without shame and guilt, and you will imagine a very unsafe, chaotic place where people are free to act out against one another without any moral inhibitions. As you can see, shame and guilt can be appropriate and healthy emotions which help us to follow rules and standards that keep our society safe. They are signals which help us to explore ourselves and our actions.

Excessive Shame and Guilt
Can Be Harmful

It is clear, however, that it is possible to have too much shame or too much guilt, and the excess of these emotions can create severe problems for the shame- or guilt-ridden individual. For some individuals, guilty thoughts dominate their every waking moment. They feel guilty and responsible for every negative event that occurs.

Take, for example, a woman named Ann, who feels excessive guilt. In nearly every situation in which she finds herself, Ann takes responsibility for whatever goes wrong, and feels that it is her fault. She is constantly overcome with guilty thoughts, and she obsesses endlessly on how she should have done things differently. Her back hurts constantly, because her muscles are continually tensed against the worry she feels, and her stomach often churns.

Her guilt feelings affect her relationships with others as well. Rather than being able to accept constructive criticism, Ann constantly defends herself to others. The people around her see her as kind of "touchy" and "sensitive," and they feel they must walk on egg shells around her. Ann's excessive guilt affects numerous different aspects of her life, including her physical health, her mental health, and her relationships with others.

Likewise, people with excessive shame continually feel badly about themselves, and usually have low self-esteem. Having grown up with parents who made negative statements about him daily, Sam has learned to have extremely shameful feelings about himself. In social situations, Sam is very fearful of being humiliated by others, as he was when he was a little boy. He carries within him impossible standards which he must meet in order to avoid feeling ashamed of himself. Sam does not realize that many of the "flaws" he perceives in himself are just part of being human.

If you suffer from excessive shame and guilt, this book is for you. In order to help you find out whether you have excessive shame or guilt, use these activities.

ACTIVITY 2:
LEARNING TO IDENTIFY EXCESSIVE SHAME IN YOURSELF

Think of a situation in which you believe you were feeling shame. Try to recall the specific details of that situation – who was there, what was said by whom, how you reacted, what you felt during and after the situation.

What was the specific situation in which you felt shame?

How did you react? Did you say anything? Was there any nonverbal body language from you (i.e., avoiding eye contact, blushing, leaving the area)?

How did you feel?

Check the feelings you experienced.

	While It Was Happening	**After It Happened**
Sad	☐	☐
Depressed	☐	☐
Small	☐	☐
Anxious	☐	☐
Embarrassed	☐	☐
Hopeless	☐	☐
Ashamed	☐	☐
Tense	☐	☐
Angry	☐	☐
Lonely	☐	☐
Guilty	☐	☐
Fearful	☐	☐
Frustrated	☐	☐
Self-Conscious	☐	☐

ACTIVITY 3:

DO YOU EXPERIENCE

EXCESSIVE SHAME?

These next few activities have been designed to help you measure the frequency, intensity, and duration of your episodes of shame. The severity of your problem with shame is reflected in how often, how intensely, and how long you suffered from shame. The greater the frequency, intensity and duration of your shame, the more likely it is that you have a problem with excessive shame. Look over your responses to the activities above, and you will get an idea of whether your shame is excessive.

Frequency: How Often Do You Feel Shame?

How often have you felt shame in the last week?

❏ Not once ❏ Once

❏ A few times ❏ Several times

❏ Every day ❏ Several times a day

If you answered that you felt shame every day or more in the past week, your shame is in the excessive range.

Intensity: How Much Shame Were You Feeling?

In the last seven days, how much have you experienced the following? Rank each one according to the level that applies to you.

0 = Not at all   1 = Somewhat
2 = Moderately   3 = A lot

____ Thinking that you are a failure

____ Wanting to hide from others

____ Feeling worthless

____ Being extremely sensitive to criticism

____ Blushing

____ Worrying obsessively about what others think of you

____ Feeling like something is wrong with you

____ Thinking that your reactions to any situation are inappropriate

Total Score: _____

If your score falls between 0-8, you have a pretty healthy sense of shame that is probably only present in situations in which it is appropriate to feel shame. If you scored within the 9-11 range, you sometimes have periods of shame, but you are able to bounce back. If your score was 12 or above, shame is a major issue for you, and the higher your score, the more excessive your shame is.

Duration: How Long After the Situation Do You Continue to Feel Shame?

After a shame-inducing situation is over, how long do you continue to feel shame?

- ☐ A Few Minutes
- ☐ 30 Minutes
- ☐ 1 Hour
- ☐ Several Hours
- ☐ All Day Long
- ☐ A Few Days
- ☐ Weeks
- ☐ Months
- ☐ A Few Years
- ☐ Many Years

Clearly, the length of time you feel shame after a situation is going to depend somewhat on how embarrassing or difficult the situation is. In some deeply humiliating situations, the recovery from shame feelings will normally take longer than if the shame-inducing situation was fleeting and somewhat less serious in nature. However, if you have shame feelings that last for days, weeks or months, that is a signal that excessive shame is a real issue for you.

Summary

Look over your responses to the frequency, intensity and duration activities above, and you will get an idea of whether or not your shame is excessive.

If you scored in the excessive range on any of the frequency, intensity and duration activities, excessive shame is a problem for you.

In the next activity, you can do a similar self-inventory regarding your experiences of guilt.

ACTIVITY 4:
LEARNING TO IDENTIFY
EXCESSIVE GUILT IN YOURSELF

Now think of a situation in which you were feeling guilt. Try to recall that specific situation in detail – who was there, what was said by whom, how you reacted, what you felt during and after the situation.

What was the specific situation in which you felt guilt?

How did you react? Did you say anything? Did you try to defend yourself or apologize excessively?

How did you feel?

	While It Was Happening	**After It Happened**
Sad	☐	☐
Depressed	☐	☐
Small	☐	☐
Anxious	☐	☐
Embarrassed	☐	☐
Hopeless	☐	☐
Ashamed	☐	☐
Tense	☐	☐
Angry	☐	☐
Lonely	☐	☐
Guilty	☐	☐
Fearful	☐	☐
Frustrated	☐	☐
Self-Conscious	☐	☐

ACTIVITY 5:

DO YOU EXPERIENCE

EXCESSIVE GUILT?

The next few activities will take you through an exploration process like the one you just completed regarding shame. This time you will be looking at the frequency, intensity, and duration of your guilt experiences. Once again, the greater the frequency, intensity and duration of your guilt experiences, the more likely it is that you have a problem with excessive guilt.

Frequency: How Often Do You Feel Guilt?

How often have you felt guilt in the last week?

❐ Not once   ❐ Once
❐ A few times   ❐ Several times
❐ Every day   ❐ Several times a day

If you answered that you felt guilt every day or more in the past week, your guilt is in the excessive range.

Intensity: How Much Guilt Do You Feel?

In the last seven days, how much have you experienced the following? Rank each one according to the level that applies to you.

0 = Not at all   1 = Somewhat
2 = Moderately   3 = A lot

_____ Having obsessive thoughts that you've done something wrong.

_____ Wishing you would have done things differently.

_____ Feeling like you should be punished.

_____ Punishing yourself by not eating or not taking care of yourself.

_____ Thinking about mistakes you made years ago.

_____ Blaming yourself when it isn't your fault.

_____ Defending yourself excessively when others try to give you feedback.

_____ Always apologizing.

_____ Feeling extremely anxious and worried.

_____ Inability to tolerate others being angry at you.

_____ Feeling that you are being selfish.

Total Score:_____

If your score falls between 0-11, you have a healthy amount of guilt that is probably only present in situations in which it is appropriate to feel guilt. If you scored within the 12-14 range, you sometimes have periods of guilt, but you are able to bounce back. If your score was 15 or above, guilt is a major issue for you, and the higher your score, the more excessive your guilt is.

After a guilt-inducing situation is over, how long do you continue to feel guilty?

❏	A Few Minutes	❏	30 Minutes
❏	1 Hour	❏	Several Hours
❏	All Day Long	❏	A Few Days
❏	Weeks	❏	Months
❏	A Few Years	❏	Many Years

The length of time you feel guilt depends on the seriousness of the situation, whether you feel that harm was done, how other people may have reacted, and a number of other factors. However, if you have done all that is humanly possible to correct the situation, and yet continue to have guilt feelings that last for months or years, clearly you need to put some attention toward understanding and reducing your excessive and punishing guilt feelings.

Summary

Look over your responses to the frequency, intensity and duration activities above, and you will get an idea of whether or not your guilt is excessive.

If you scored in the excessive range on any of the frequency, intensity and duration activities, excessive guilt is a problem for you.

The use of the activities in this book, the help of a professional psychotherapist, and the support of friends and loved ones can help you to free yourself from this painful burden.

Now that you have a basic understanding of shame and guilt, and you have learned to identify excessive shame and guilt, you may find yourself asking the common question, "Why me?"

In Chapters 2 and 3, the origins of excessive shame and guilt are explained so that you can get an idea of why it is that you have developed excessive shame or guilt.

PART 2

HOW DID WE COME TO
HAVE SHAME AND GUILT?

CHAPTER 2

CULTURAL SOURCES OF SHAME AND GUILT

Culture and Society

We all grow up in the context of our culture. It surrounds us every day, and it shapes the values we hold, and the way we dress, speak, interact, and feel about ourselves. It even affects how we treat one another as individuals. More specifically, our culture tells us what human characteristics are shameful, and what behaviors should cause us guilt. Although these cultural rules can be positive in their ability to guide us towards morally appropriate behavior such as avoiding harming others, they can also be damaging to us.

The culture around us tells us that certain characteristics, such as being female or of a certain ethnic background or age bracket, are shameful. As we spend our childhood years being exposed to these ideas and values, we gradually internalize them, and they become a part of our beliefs and values. When we find that we ourselves may have some of these characteristics, or may act in some of the ways that our culture sees as unacceptable, we develop shame or guilt internally. These feelings of shame and guilt punish us when we step outside the bounds of our culture's expectations. We can grow up feeling that we are worthless or unacceptable because of those parts of who we are, and we become incapable of loving ourselves as unique human beings.

Although we may assert passionately that "all men are created equal," in actual practice, the culture in which we live may make us very intolerant of differences between us. Instead of celebrating differences among people, we learn to fear and dislike people who are different from us either in who they are or how they behave. Consider a child, Eric, who is teased in school because he is overweight. If we truly believed that differences were what made the world go round, Eric would be treated the same way as any other child. But, instead, the message which Eric receives is that there is something wrong with him and that is why no one likes him. Eric learns to feel ashamed of himself as a person, and he learns to feel intense guilt whenever he eats.

When we start to become aware of ways in which our cultural values promote shame and guilt, we can then begin to understand our own feelings of shame and guilt, and we can make positive changes in our lives to reduce excessive feelings of shame and guilt. No matter who you are or what you do, our society probably has a value or rule which negatively influences how others view you or treat you. Cultural values affect everyone, not just a particular minority group.

For example, consider the rule that men are not supposed to cry. What if a man does cry? He may feel deep shame about the fact that he cried because he is afraid of being viewed as weak and unmanly. In a large number of cultures, from the time they are very young, boys are consistently humiliated by others for crying. Crying is a normal, healthy human expression of emotion, and yet boys are often severely punished or shamed for doing it. Boys are usually made to feel guilty for having cried because they have somehow disappointed the expectations of their parents (especially their fathers).

As we will explore in the next section, there are several other groups of people who are subjected to humiliation, discrimination or mistreatment because of who they are or what they do.

Prejudices and How They Damage Us

Sexism

There are many ways in which sexism affects both men and women by dictating narrow rules of what is acceptable for each gender. Fay and Robert, a married couple with two children, provide a good illustration of how guilt and shame can occur when people stray outside the rigid gender roles prescribed by their culture. After the birth of their second child, Robert injured himself at work and was no longer able to stay in his construction job. Together they decided that Fay would go back to her nursing job while Robert provided child care at home and managed the house. Both of them found that they adjusted well to this change in roles and came to feel comfortable in their different domains.

However, both Fay and Robert found themselves feeling shame and guilt at times. Fay felt guilty that she wasn't at home with her children more, and Robert found that he felt ashamed of being a "house husband" whenever he talked with his friends. In addition, Robert felt guilt that he wasn't being a "good provider" for his family. Although both members of the couple actually enjoyed and adapted to their new roles, they sometimes suffered extreme guilt and shame, especially when they were confronted with other people who did not approve of their new roles.

The worst incident for Robert happened when he went to a parent-teacher conference for his daughter Louisa, and the teacher said, "Who are you? I was expecting to meet with Louisa's mother." He felt embarrassed and angry as he explained that he was the one in charge of child care in the family.

Racism

Racial prejudice is another part of our culture that damages our ability to love and accept ourselves as we are. Exactly how does racism do this to us? Here are a few instances shared by Terrie, an African-American woman in her mid-20s. She recalls walking one day in a predominantly Caucasian neighborhood. A car drove by slowly and a voice yelled out, "Nigger!"

Terrie says, "At first, I just felt angry, but a few hours later, I noticed how hard it was for me to feel good about myself after an incident like that." Instead of feeling pride in her heritage, she felt ashamed of who she is.

Terrie adds, "As I looked at myself in the mirror later that day, I remembered another painful time, when my aunt told me I was too 'dark,' and that I should try to date only light-skinned boys in order to 'lighten' up the family. That really hurt."

These messages of racism from inside and outside the African-American community have caused her pain and shame about who she is.

Homophobia

Homophobia in our culture also creates shame and guilt. Eli, a gay man, relates that the homophobia around him has become such a part of him that whenever he talks to his parents about his relationship with a man, he feels very guilty. His parents are openly critical of him being gay, and they sometimes tell him how much embarrassment he causes them.

Although he believes that his relationship with his partner, Rick, is the best thing that has ever happened to him, and he has been with Rick for over ten years, he continues to be plagued with guilt.

Rather than valuing the good things in his life, he continually questions himself, thinking that he really shouldn't be living this life. Rather than feeling self-respect, Eli struggles with guilt feelings. In fact, he feels guilty whenever he goes out with his partner because he feels like he is doing something wrong. The homophobia within and around him forces him to stay home all the time and remain "in the closet."

Ageism

Ageism makes it very hard for aging adults to feel good about themselves. Most of us do not realize how widespread this attitude is until we have experienced it ourselves. However, you do not need to look far to discover instances of ageism. If you turn on your television, you will see ad after ad for products that remove signs of aging, such as wrinkles. Beyond these widely broadcast negative attitudes about aging, many older adults experience discrimination because of their age.

Many organizations make cutbacks and save money by laying off older, more experienced employees with high salaries and hiring younger, less experienced employees at much lower salaries. Many older adults find it difficult to find jobs after a certain age, even if they are more than qualified for the job. When these experiences occur in our culture, older adults receive shaming messages that they are useless because they are old, or guilt-inducing messages that they are nothing but a burden to others.

People with HIV/AIDS

Prejudices tend to grow out of our fear of people who are different from us. A prime example of this type of fear is the prejudice against people who are living with HIV or AIDS. There are many ways in which this type of fear can be expressed, and when people become

THE SPIRAL OF SHAME

afraid enough, they begin to discriminate against others. Frank, whose Kaposi's sarcoma lesions made his AIDS diagnosis very visible, shared the following experience of discrimination that led him to feel shame about his condition.

"I saw an ad in the newspaper for an apartment, so I called and spoke with the landlord on the phone. The landlord said that the apartment was available. We really hit it off on the phone and the landlord said that the apartment was basically all but mine, as long as I came over today and filled out an application. When I met the landlord in person, he asked me why I had red blotches on my face, and I told him it was a skin rash from too much sun. He gave me an odd look and asked if I had AIDS or something. I asked him if it would matter if I did have AIDS, and he just stared at me and finally said that he had forgotten that the apartment was already rented. I felt terrible afterwards, like I was too unworthy to live in that apartment or anywhere else for that matter."

This experience of discrimination left Frank feeling hopeless and ashamed. He only started to feel better when he got angry and decided to investigate legal action against the landlord.

ACTIVITY 1:

IDENTIFYING EXPERIENCES OF PREJUDICE OR DISCRIMINATION LEADING TO SHAME AND GUILT

There are many groups of individuals who feel that they are not worthy or are defective as a result of experiences of discrimination in our culture. Reflect on your own experiences.

Have there been times in your life when you felt you were treated badly because of prejudice? Describe those experiences.

How do you think those experiences have affected you? How did they make you feel at the time?

Are there any specific groups of people with whom you don't feel very comfortable, or for whom you feel dislike? Here is a partial list of some groups of people who are often targets of prejudice or discrimination. Check any group with which you usually feel uncomfortable.

☐ Elderly

☐ Bisexual

☐ Women

☐ Homosexual

☐ In recovery or chemically dependent

☐ Differently-abled or challenged

☐ African-American

☐ Overweight

☐ Asian

☐ HIV+ or AIDS

☐ Hispanic

☐ Native American

☐ Latino

☐ Jewish or other religions

☐ Puerto Rican

☐ People on Welfare

☐ Cuban

☐ Other

Think about any areas in which you might have prejudices. Generally our discomfort with a group arises because we don't know much about that group. We tend to fear the unknown.

Now, commit yourself to taking the time to learn more about this group.

Indirect Experiences of Prejudice and Discrimination

Prejudice can come in many forms. It can be direct – like losing a job because of your gender, or being teased for being overweight. However, differential treatment or prejudice can take much more subtle forms such as jokes.

For example, consider how many jokes are circulating in our culture about Polish people. How do Polish people feel every time they hear yet another "Polack joke?"

When we are insulted or ridiculed because of who we are, shame and guilt will naturally arise.

ACTIVITY 2:

IDENTIFYING INDIRECT FORMS OF

PREJUDICE AND DISCRIMINATION

YOU HAVE EXPERIENCED

Remembering the last party you attended, did you hear any jokes that were "put-downs" for any group listed here? Check all that apply.

- ❑ Elderly
- ❑ Bisexual
- ❑ Women
- ❑ Homosexual
- ❑ In recovery or chemically dependent
- ❑ Differently-abled or challenged
- ❑ African-American
- ❑ Overweight
- ❑ Asian
- ❑ HIV+ or AIDS
- ❑ Hispanic
- ❑ Native American
- ❑ Latino
- ❑ Jewish or other religions
- ❑ Puerto Rican
- ❑ People on Welfare
- ❑ Cuban
- ❑ Other

How did the joking make you feel?

How did you react when you heard this type of insult? Did you say anything to anyone or did you laugh with everyone else?

Have you ever been present when someone insulted a group of which you were a member? How did that make you feel?

What would you do differently if it happened again?

Special Populations Who Struggle with Shame and Guilt

People with Religious Guilt and Shame

For many people, religion is a very positive and helpful experience. However, there are some people who have experienced forms of religion that left them feeling like a "bad" person, or that they were unworthy as a human being. They may be riddled with guilt not only about what they may have done, but about how much more good they should have done. One young man shares his experiences with religious guilt and shame.

Alan calls himself a "recovering Catholic." He describes his experience with religious guilt in the following way: "I was always getting in trouble at the religious school I attended as a youngster. Whenever I misbehaved or broke a rule, all I remember is being told I was going to go to Hell when I was punished. I was frequently told that I was very bad when I broke a rule, and I grew up believing that I must be a bad person. Especially, I was taught that any sexual thought was a sin and dirty. Now I have a hard time enjoying sex with my wife, and I feel dirty for days afterwards."

In order to explore whether or not religious guilt or shame are issues for you, try the next activity.

ACTIVITY 3:
YOUR EXPERIENCES WITH
RELIGIOUS GUILT OR SHAME

Remembering your experiences when you were actively participating in a religion that taught you about shame and guilt, what were the specific things that you were told were the worst things you could do? In other words, what were the things that you learned to feel guilt or shame about? Rank each one of these different behaviors in terms of how sinful you consider them to be..

0 = Not at all   1 = Somewhat
2 = Moderately   3 = A lot

_____ Killing someone

_____ Hurting someone

_____ Having sex outside of marriage

_____ Having sex under any circumstances

_____ Eating foods that are outside your religion's dietary restrictions

_____ Marrying someone outside of your faith

_____ Thinking lustful thoughts

_____ Disobeying your parents

_____ Spending money on yourself

_____ Smoking cigarettes

_____ Taking drugs

_____ Drinking alcohol

_____ Coming home after curfew

_____ Masturbation

_____ Sexual foreplay

_____ Sex with a person of the same gender

_____ Cutting your hair short (for women)

_____ Growing your hair long (for men)

_____ Swearing

_____ Not attending religious services

_____ Using contraception

_____ Having an abortion

_____ Not dressing according to your religion's rules of dress

_____ Other

The purpose of this exercise is to clarify in your own mind which behaviors you would link with shame and guilt.

Of course, some religious laws help us to learn ethical and moral behavior. However, there may be some which you might now question.

Do you remember any instances of an adult shaming or humiliating you for these behaviors or any others not listed? If so, what did they say or do?

How did you react?

How has this religious shame or guilt affected your actions or how you feel about yourself?

Shame and Guilt and Addiction Issues

Many people who have problems with drugs, alcohol or other addictions have feelings of shame and guilt. Because addictions can lead people to do things that hurt others, it can sometimes be difficult to separate healthy guilt about these issues from unhealthy guilt. Along with the guilt, you can also feel shame about your inability to control your addictive behavior. Most people who have never struggled with these issues have little understanding of what a challenge it is to recover from addictions, and their judgmental attitudes towards your addiction can make the guilt and shame much worse.

Addictions can fill you with such guilt and shame that you may find yourself driven back to your addictive behavior in order to escape from these feelings. Of course, this way of coping only leads to even more shame and guilt.

How do you escape this vicious cycle of addiction and shame and guilt?

Rod, a recovering alcoholic, shares his experiences of becoming free of shame and guilt through his recovery from his addiction. "For years, deep inside I knew that I was hurting people, destroying my marriage, neglecting my kids, and a lot of other things. Every time I'd stop and look at my life, which was seldom, since I tried to stay drunk to avoid this, I felt ashamed of myself, and I felt bad about everything that I did. I found out, though, that the way to recovery isn't through shame or guilt. I didn't become sober because I finally felt guilty enough. I became sober because I found the tiniest corner of me that cared about what happened to me. Once I got sober I faced all those things that I had done that had hurt other people, and I apologized and tried to make amends to everyone I'd ever hurt. I can't tell you how much pride and self-respect I felt when I had completed that process. Because others forgave me, I became able to forgive myself, and let go of my guilt and shame."

Rod's experience shows us that there is a freedom that waits for us beyond the shame and guilt we now have.

If you have an addiction, whether it involves drugs, alcohol, food, spending, sex, gambling or any other type of addictive behavior, stop listening to the part of you that is "beating you up" with guilt or shame.

Instead, find that voice of self-respect in you that cares enough to seek help.

ACTIVITY 4:

ADDICTIONS AND FEELINGS OF SHAME AND GUILT

Do you struggle with any addictions? Check any that apply to you below, and add any of your own.

- ☐ Recreational drugs
- ☐ Prescription drugs
- ☐ Alcohol
- ☐ Sexual activity
- ☐ Food
- ☐ Gambling
- ☐ Spending
- ☐ Other

Are you currently getting help for any of these addictions?

Do you currently know anyone you could call on who would be supportive of you being in recovery, such as someone else in recovery?

Do you have anyone in your life who shames you or criticizes you for having an addiction? If so, what does this person say that makes you feel shame or guilt?

When do you usually experience this shame or guilt? In what kinds of situations?

How has this addiction-related shame or guilt affected you? How has it affected your actions or how you feel about yourself or others?

Conclusion

When we are treated differently or discriminated against in our culture, there is a clear message from our society that we are less than worthy human beings. When being yourself is not socially acceptable, you can begin to feel shame or guilt about who you are or what you do. Whether you are treated differently or unfairly because you are older, Hispanic, differently-abled, gay, or Jewish does not really matter. What does matter is that when we are treated as second class citizens, eventually these messages lead to feelings of shame about who we are or guilt about what we do.

When we see instances of discrimination or prejudice against ourselves or others occurring, we can fight back against it by speaking up. By deciding to speak up, we make a commitment to stopping ourselves and others from being damaged by shame and guilt. We can also commit to providing support for those who are being shamed or who suffer from excessive guilt. Whether we become involved on a personal, a community or a more global political level, each small thing we do can help us transform our corner of the world into a more just and compassionate place.

CHAPTER 3

FAMILY OF ORIGIN ISSUES AND THE DEVELOPMENT OF SHAME AND GUILT

How Shame and Guilt Entered Your Life

The Impact of the Family

Not only do societal attitudes affect your sense of shame and guilt, but attitudes that existed in the family as you grew up also affect these feelings.

This family in which you grew up is often referred to as your family of origin. The attitudes in this family were the very first ones you encountered when you were developing a sense of who you are in the world.

Before you were able to know that it was possible to have different attitudes, your family's attitudes were the ones to which you were exposed. It makes sense that these attitudes would have a profound impact on you throughout your life, even well into adulthood.

You may not even be aware of the ways in which you are currently influenced by the experiences and attitudes that surrounded you when you were a child.

The purpose of this section on your family of origin is to help you become personally aware, through information and activities, of the ways in which shame and guilt may have entered into your life. Although your painful feelings of shame and guilt may have entered your life through your family of origin, these two emotions enter your life through different pathways.

That is, people who struggle mostly with shame feelings generally have had a different set of experiences with their family of origin than those who struggle with guilt feelings. In order to understand these experiences, it is important to look at your family of origin as a whole.

Your Family Environment as a System

One of the most helpful ways of looking at a family of origin is to view it as a system in which all of the members affect one another. In a system like this, sometimes the ways in which family members affect each other may not be particularly healthy for the individual members or for the family as a whole. Shame and guilt can pervade a whole family, and certain types of family styles tend to be associated with shame or guilt.

Let us look first at how shame develops and operates in a family system, and then how guilt evolves and shapes a family system. In both cases, we will look at how these families produce shame-prone or guilt-prone adults.

Shame in the Family System

Shame in families is not an all-or-nothing thing. That is, some families have a high degree of shame in them, sometimes so much that we call these families shame-bound. In contrast, some families have very little shame in them, and we call these families respectful families. Rather than struggling with painful shame feelings, people who grow up in respectful families naturally develop a sense of self-respect and pride.

There are a number of ways in which shame-bound families differ from respectful families. According to Fossum and Mason (1986), shame-bound families are like "peanut brittle, with each person fixed in stereo-typed, inflexible roles and relationships to one anoth-er...when change exerts enough force all at one moment upon a rigid system, it may break and splin-ter" (p. 19). Any kind of change is going to increase the stress in the family, and change tends to be seen as very threatening.

As an illustration, consider Fred, who comes from a shame-bound family in which his mother is a shaming and domineering force. No one in the family dares to confront or even disagree with the mother in this family, because she answers any disagreement with a personal attack on the person who has confronted her.

For example, when Fred's sister Abbey tried to stand up to their mother, their mother put her down by saying disrespectful things that made Abbey feel ashamed of herself.

After Fred spends some time in psychotherapy exploring why he feels ashamed when he tries to stand up to other people, he discovers that the root of this problem lies in his difficulty standing up to his intimidating mother.

The next time he attends a family gathering, rather than agreeing with his mother during discussions as the rest of the family does, he quietly begins to assert his own opinions. He stands up to his mother, and does not change his stated views when challenged by her.

This family has learned to live by a strict set of rules imposed by the mother. The main rule goes something like this: Don't challenge or disagree with Mom or you will suffer the consequences. By asserting his own opinions, Fred breaks this family rule and the other family members become quiet and nervous.

After the gathering, the other family members call each other and talk about how inappropriate Fred's behavior was, and wonder who he thinks he is, after all. There is no direct discussion of the incident with Fred, just secrets between other family members.

There is no flexibility in this system to tolerate differing opinions, and so whoever attempts to "rock the boat" ends up being shamed by the other members of the family. Their only option is to place Fred outside the accepting circle of the family, and show silent, shaming disapproval. The next time they have a family gathering, they might "forget" to invite Fred.

In contrast, a respectful family system has the capacity to absorb change in its members and still stay connected. Differences in opinion between members are accepted and embraced. Members of the family communicate openly with each other, and are sometimes vulnerable and dependent on each other for support. Differences are discussed openly and members do not "manage their relationships with secrets" (Fossum & Mason, 1987, p. 20).

Let's consider the previous example involving Fred and imagine how it might be different if he came from a family which was more on the respectful end of the continuum.

Perhaps his mother might still be somewhat domineering, but when challenged, she could tolerate it better and listen to him rather than treating his opinion as a threat to her power. Therefore, she would not feel the need to shame Fred or make him look silly in front of other family members.

This approach would lead to less tension and stress for the whole family. Family members would not feel the need to take sides and shun the person who has the different opinion. Instead, these differences could be passionately argued among all family members without a sense of shame or injury occurring in any one of them. For the next family gathering, they would remember to invite Fred.

Often the real-life experiences of people in shame-bound families are far more dramatic and painful than the ones Fred experienced. Shame-bound families have a tendency to keep secrets and to not communicate freely about what is really happening.

When family members don't feel that they can be honest with each other because they are ashamed, the entire family can simply deny that there is ever anything wrong. Family members can be disrespected, or even verbally, physically or sexually abused, and no one ever objects.

Family members may feel so ashamed and so bad about themselves that they never find the courage to voice their feelings to each other or anyone else.

Consider Arlene who found herself feeling intense anger towards her father after family gatherings because she would watch him verbally abusing her mother, calling her terrible names. At the same time, she felt such profound shame that she continually questioned her feelings of anger, and tended to mini-mize them. She would think to herself, "Hmm. I felt so uncomfortable watching my father at the last family gathering. Nobody else seemed to notice though, so it must have just been me."

In shame-bound families all sorts of hurtful and destructive activities can occur, with everyone in the family supporting the continuation of those activities by their silence. Spouses can regularly become violent with each other, and then the next day act as if nothing has occurred.

When a parent in a shame-bound family has a serious drinking problem, a child might ask the other parent what is happening. The answer may be, "Your mother is sick" or "she's just in one of her moods." This response is the equivalent of silence, twisting the truth quite a bit to keep the secret.

The underlying shaming message to the child is do not trust your feelings of discomfort at seeing your mother drunk on a regular basis.

This type of message leads children straight down the path of shame in that when they do have feelings that they have learned are unacceptable to their parents, they become ashamed of their feelings.

These are the ways in which shame-bound families sacrifice the well-being of the individuals for the sake of maintaining family secrets and avoiding being shamed by other family members.

ACTIVITY 1:
IDENTIFYING SHAMING MESSAGES
YOU RECEIVED IN YOUR FAMILY

Here are some of the symptoms associated with experiencing intense shame. Check off any symptoms that you remember feeling as a child, and reflect on these symptoms as you answer the questions.

❐ Blushing

❐ Wanting to hide from others

❐ Feeling like you are not completely present

❐ Feeling "spaced out"

❐ Feeling like something is wrong with you

❐ Feeling worthless

❐ Feeling your heart pounding

❐ Feeling your palms sweating

❐ Thinking your reactions to a situation are not appropriate

❐ Thinking that you are a failure

❐ Feeling extreme sensitivity to criticism

❐ Feeling excessively concerned about the opinions of others

❐ Not trusting your feelings or instincts

Can you identify any situations in your childhood in which you felt intense shame? List as
many of these situations as you can.

Do you notice any patterns or commonalities
between the different situations you listed? For
example, did they all happen in your home, or
at school, or with one particular family member?

Do you remember any specific shaming statements made about you by family members?
Write them down.

Do you remember any specific actions taken by your family members which led you to feel ashamed? Check all that apply.

- ❐ Laughing at you
- ❐ Ignoring you
- ❐ Calling you obscene names
- ❐ Talking about some physical feature of yours
- ❐ Talking about you behind your back
- ❐ Embarrassing you in front of your friends
- ❐ Sharing things you asked to be kept secret
- ❐ Criticizing you in front of people that are important to you (friends, grandparents, teachers, coaches)
- ❐ Other things that have happened to you

How many of these shaming statements and actions continue to happen in your family, even during your adulthood?

Rules in Shame-Bound Families

Shame-bound families tend to operate by a specific set of rules that protect the family from the threat of change (Fossum & Mason, 1986). Of course, change can be positive or negative, in that sometimes change destroys families and sometimes it makes them grow closer and stronger. In order to prevent any negative changes or threats to the family, these rules lead families to avoid all changes period, including healthy changes. The rules are never really articulated in the family; instead, they are learned through repeated interactions between members. Most members of the family would probably not even be aware that these rules are operating, because the rules have become so habitual over the years.

The most important rule of all is this one: Make sure to have control of your own behavior and of the behavior others. In other words, control all interactions with other people. According to Fossum and Mason (1986), "the control principle is motivated not so much by a drive to power as by a drive for predictability and safety. Spontaneity and surprise are threats within this system and interaction is characterized by manipulation rather than domination" (pp. 88-89).

Edmund comes from a shaming family. He tries to control his family whenever they are together by planning out an itinerary of activities for all of the family members to follow. The purpose of this tight schedule is to avoid any sort of spontaneous activity that might possibly get out of control. Edmund has learned that with his family, any unplanned time could produce a number of problems. Dad might start drinking, or mom might start a public shouting match with Edmund's brother about his career plans.

Edmund is convinced that there is something very wrong with his family, and with him. He always hopes that if he just provides a way to keep everyone busy, he can avoid embarrassing scenes, and therefore avoid feeling shame about being a part of his family. The activity schedules he makes up are his way of trying to make the family safe.

Another important rule of shame-bound families is the perfection rule. The people who grow up in this family learn that it is absolutely unacceptable to make mistakes. People who grow up under the perfection rule learn that if you make an error, there is obviously something wrong with you.

These individuals grow up thinking in very black and white stereotypes; they believe that there is one right way and one wrong way, and if they are not right, they are deeply ashamed. They continually criticize themselves and feel unworthy in nearly everything they do, because perfection is an impossible standard.

This rule serves nearly the same function as the control rule in that it provides predictability to the family, even though it develops destructive self-hatred within the individual members.

Denial also characterizes shame-bound families. Webster's dictionary defines denial as "a refusal to believe or accept" (p. 166).

Denial of family problems such as physical or sexual abuse, alcoholism, drug dependence, or mental illness allows the family to go on without having to confront painful issues for which they may have no immediate solution.

Often the denial is so strong that any family member who challenges the family's denial will be treated with disrespect, and made to feel like an outsider.

Another family rule which reinforces and supports all of the ones above is the "no-talk rule." This rule involves keeping family conversations on a superficial level and never talking about real concerns.

Often members of shame-bound families will go for years without stating a vulnerable feeling or a controversial point of view to another family member.

To illustrate how this no-talk rule is enforced within the family, let's look at Katie, whose stepfather, Hal, makes sexually inappropriate comments to her about her rear end and breasts. When Hal makes these comments, Katie feels intensely disrespected, ashamed, uncomfortable, and angry.

One day she brings up the subject of Hal's comments while talking with her older sister Jodi. She tells Jodi how completely embarrassed and angry she feels when Hal inappropriately makes sexual comments regarding her body parts. Jodi replies, "Oh, that's not a big deal. That's just the way men are. Don't worry about it."

Katie wonders if there is something wrong with her, because this issue does not bother her older sister. Katie sits in silence feeling even more ashamed for having brought up the issue with her sister.

Her sister supports the no-talk rule by telling Katie in so many words not to talk about this issue. In addition, her sister also shows her own denial about the inappropriate things that go on in the family.

ACTIVITY 2:
IDENTIFYING SHAMING RULES
IN YOUR FAMILY OF ORIGIN

As you reflect on these next questions, think back to how it was for you, as you were growing up in your family.

CONTROL

Did any of your family members work hard at controlling what happened in your family? Did one family member always insist on having things his or her own way? For example, did anyone plan activities in great detail?

Did anyone in your family attempt to control conversations by interrupting, or not allowing other members to have private conversations?

Did you ever see your parents try to control each other or other family members through threats of harm, or through physical intimidation or abuse?

PERFECTION

What was the usual response from your parents when you made a mistake? Were you criticized? Were you punished?

Were you told that you were incapable of doing things correctly, or made to feel that somehow you weren't good enough?

Did you see other family members being punished either verbally or physically for making mistakes?

How did your parents deal with you when you were unable to do something? Was their response patient and supportive or did they react with frustration or anger?

DENIAL

When something about your family bothered
you, how did your parents or siblings react?
Were you able to discuss it openly with them?
Did they ever refuse to believe you?

How did family members respond when you
expressed difficult feelings such as anger or
sadness?

When you brought up something that really
bothered you, can you recall ever receiving a
response from a family member that minimized
or made light of it? What did they say?

NO TALK RULE

Did any family member ever forbid you to talk about a family problem, or in any other way make you feel that it was shameful or inappropriate to discuss the problem?

When you talk about family problems with family members as an adult, how do you feel?

☐ Nervous

☐ Embarrassed

☐ Ashamed

☐ Comfortable

☐ Relaxed

☐ Guilty

☐ Sad

☐ Angry

☐ Neutral

☐ Calm

☐ Frustrated

☐ Other

Parental Influences

As we grew up, our interactions with our parents were the strongest influence that shaped our feelings about ourselves. Seeing ourselves through our parents' eyes, we form impressions of who we are that will stay with us for the rest of our lives. Unfortunately, parents have all of the same subjective likes and dislikes for certain types of people that all humans have, and sometimes their children don't become the kind of people they can easily connect with and enjoy.

For example, Aaron is not very good at sports. Aaron's father has a very strong desire for his son to "follow in his footsteps" in terms of being a star athlete. Deeply disappointed in his son, Aaron's father frequently says, "I cannot believe I have such a wimpy son!" He also doesn't spend much time with Aaron, because he gets irritated at his son's lack of athletic ability. Aaron hears this type of statement about himself, and he comes to believe that he is a failure as a person. He believes that he has failed in the only way that matters.

We can see how shame can develop from hearing critical statements from parents. However, shame can also develop in response to nonverbal messages of rejection. Imagine that Aaron's father never says anything about his disappointment in his son. Instead, he just ignores Aaron, hoping that his son won't notice the lack of attention. Rather than focusing on his disappointment in Aaron, he spends his time with Aaron's athletic younger brother, Stephen. With Stephen, he feels happy and proud, because he believes that all of his talents are reflected in this son. Aaron frequently watches Stephen and his father outside practicing pitching and batting, and feels ashamed that he isn't more like Stephen.

What could Aaron's father do differently to change the family environment to a less shaming one? Obviously, he can't completely change his feelings of disappointment. However, aside from not expressing those feelings, he could also spend more time with Aaron, helping him discover other interests that he can do well, and that he enjoys. If he were to take this approach, Aaron would receive the message that even though he may not excel at sports, he is still worthy and loved.

Guilt in the Family System

Excessive guilt feelings develop in much the same way as shame feelings, with one crucial difference. Guilt feelings come from experiences of being blamed for something you may have done, rather than something you are. Children who are excessively criticized for their actions grow up blaming themselves for everything, and feel a deep sense of guilt. There are a number of different types of family characteristics which can predispose you towards becoming an excessively guilty person.

In our families of origin, we learn about something called boundaries. In the physical world, boundaries have to do with where one thing begins and another thing ends. For example, a property you own has boundaries. There is a place where that property ends, and your neighbors' property begins. As we grow up in our families of origin, we learn about boundaries between people. Every family has a different sense of where one person ends and the other begins. We learn at a young age that mom and dad are separate from us, and not an extension of our bodies.

We may also learn that just as our bodies are separate from each other, so are our emotions and experiences. That is, we can learn that when mommy is upset there may be reasons that we don't understand that cause her to be upset. This is an important lesson, because if we never develop a sense of boundaries – of where we stop and the other person begins - we are likely to have numerous emotional difficulties with guilt in which we blame ourselves for the feelings or actions of others.

In some families with poor boundaries, everybody is so connected with everyone else that when one person becomes upset, everyone is upset. There is a ripple effect that spreads throughout the family. All of the family members ask themselves what they did to upset the other family member. In such a family, a child grows up learning to have an unhealthy, exaggerated sense of responsibility for other people's happiness and well-being. This situation breeds high levels of guilt which continue into adulthood and extend beyond the family.

Keisha, for example, comes from an overly connected family which breeds guilt. When she starts working as an adult, she finds she is overly sensitive to everyone's moods in her workplace, and she feels personally responsible if her boss seems to be in a bad mood. Any time her boss seems upset, she looks for what she might have done to displease him and she feels extremely guilty. Luckily, she is able to talk to her boss, and is told repeatedly that when her boss is upset, it usually has absolutely nothing to do with her.

How exactly is this lack of boundaries and sense of guilt learned in a family? Sometimes we learn this directly through our parents talking to us, and other times we learn it indirectly through nonverbal messages such as a disapproving or angry look. Thus, we don't learn to assign responsibility correctly, and don't learn appropriate boundaries.

Consider a young child, Suzy, whose mother is slamming cupboard doors, which gets Suzy's attention, and conveys the message that mommy is very angry. Suzy's mom does not tell Suzy why she is so upset. Suzy starts to wonder if perhaps she did something wrong, because her mother is slamming cabinet doors in front of her and giving her the silent treatment. Suzy starts to feel guilty, believing that she must have done something wrong to anger her mother so much.

Before Suzy realizes it, she has indirectly received a message from her mother, which she now interprets in such a way that she feels guilty whenever people around her are upset and silent.

To be more specific, poor boundaries can lead to excessive guilt by leading you to the misperception that you can cause certain feelings in others, while blinding you to what the other person brings to the situation. After all, because the other person is a separate human being, he or she brings a unique set of experiences, likes, dislikes, and vulnerabilities.

Whereas Suzy's mother was conveying an indirect guilt- inducing message, some parents communicate the message more directly through words. A more direct guilt-inducing example is Teresa, a 9-year-old girl, whose mother suffers from bouts of severe depression. Her mother has been hospitalized several times for her depression, and the entire family has had to adjust their behavior in order to avoid upsetting her.

Teresa's mother is extremely hypersensitive, and tends to misinterpret other people's actions. One day Teresa decides to wear a different dress to school than the one her mother wants her to wear. When her mother sees her in the other dress, she leaves the room and goes into her bedroom and cries for an hour. Teresa's father, giving a direct message, angrily says to Teresa, "Jesus, look what you did to your mom! Now I'm going to have to try to calm her down for the rest of the day while you're off at school!"

For the rest of the day, Teresa believes she has caused her mother's distress and has such a profound sense of guilt and self-hatred that she can't concentrate on anything in her classes. Because Teresa's mother often does not feel very comfortable with Teresa, she gets blamed for a lot of her mother's "moods." As an adult, Teresa often has trouble discerning when things are her fault; she tends to take responsibility for most of the negative events around her.

How could that situation have been handled by Teresa's father in a way that would have been less guilt-inducing?

Teresa's father could have sat down with her and explained that her mother's moods can be set off by many different things, and that Teresa did not do anything wrong. He could have told her that he loves her, and that Teresa's mother loves her too, but has a lot of limitations and problems. In this way, Teresa would experience her father's acceptance of her and her actions, and she would not develop inappropriate guilt.

ACTIVITY 3:

IDENTIFYING WEAK BOUNDARIES
IN YOUR FAMILY OF ORIGIN

It is important to identify poor or weak boundaries in order to understand the origins of our
excessive guilt. In this activity, you will explore
how the boundaries in your family may have
been blurred or weak.

Remember a few situations when you inappropriately took on the feelings which belonged to
other family members.

How did that make you feel?

Whose feelings were you really taking responsibility for?

Can you describe any situations as an adult in which you were so sensitive to others' feelings that you took responsibility for another person's feelings and felt guilty?

What kinds of feelings do you usually shoulder or take the responsibility for in people around you? Check all that apply.

☐ Sadness
☐ Happiness
☐ Shame
☐ Anxiety
☐ Fear
.☐ Guilt
☐ Sadness
☐ Anger
☐ Frustration
☐ Other

Perfectionism

Another way in which you may have learned to think in guilt-inducing ways is by being in a highly perfectionistic family. In these types of families, there is a belief that you can be perfect if you just try hard enough. Mistakes are inexcusable in this family, and everything you do must meet a very high and sometimes impossible standard. In this family, there is no such thing as "partial credit" for getting most of it right. You have either succeeded or failed, with nothing in between. Thus, when you fall short of perfection, you feel guilty as though you have done something wrong and failed.

You may have grown up in a family in which you were expected to do things that were nearly impossible for someone your age. Perhaps you were asked to take care of younger children at an age when you would not have known how to handle emergencies or problems that could arise, and then you were criticized for not knowing what to do.

You may have been blamed when a younger sibling hurt himself or damaged property. In that case, you were actively taught to take on the responsibility and the guilt for your sibling's behavior, leaving you vulnerable to episodes of guilt throughout your life.

Some families have a very strong tendency to place blame. In these families, there is no such thing as a "no-fault" situation or a misunderstanding. Let's look at Lisa's family as an example, in which her father blamed everyone around him.

For years, Lisa watched her father beat up her mother and listened to him blame her mother for it. He would say, "You know when you make me mad you make me have to hit you!" At first, Lisa was confused by this logic, and she wondered whether her mother had special powers to make her father's fists connect with her mother's face. How did her mom get her father to hit her, and why would she want to do that?

After many years, however, she learned to believe that her mother must be responsible for the abuse just because she made daddy mad. She learned that she had better be careful to never make her father mad. When she did occasionally do something that seemed to make her father irritated or angry, she felt extremely guilty and was very grateful that he never hit her.

In Lisa's family system, her father was protected by blaming. He was never forced to look at his own abusive behavior. He successfully diverted the attention away from his own behavior by criticizing and blaming others, and the other family members became trained to feel guilty and responsible whenever he was angry.

In some families a particular person is chosen to bear the blame for all of the family problems. This person is called the "scapegoat." This is the person onto whom the entire family can focus all their negative, blaming excuses for their own problems and failures.

Ernie was the scapegoat in his family. He became a bad kid because everybody seemed to expect him to be bad. His older brother had made prior claims to being the "perfect" kid in the family. Ernie's independent spirit made him naturally fall into being the problem child. He believed that he often created tremendous problems for his family, which left him feeling guilty.

Ernie did not realize how much he provided for his family by fulfilling his role as a scapegoat until he tried to become a responsible adult. He then became aware that because he was the family scapegoat, dad could continue drinking as much as he wanted, and when someone criticized him for his drinking, he could say, "If you had a kid like mine, you'd drink too!" Mom could continue putting off going back to school by blaming it on having to take care of Ernie.

When Ernie began to live a more independent life, he noticed that even though he was no longer the one "creating problems" for his family, his father continued to drink, and his mother never went back to school. Realizing what his scapegoat role provided for his family, Ernie then understood that he had been used as everyone else's excuse. He was finally able to let go of the deep guilt he had been carrying, as he realized that he did not keep his mother or his father from attaining their dreams and goals.

Interestingly enough, even children who are not treated as scapegoats, such as "perfect" children, can end up saddled with the burden of guilt. In contrast to the type of guilt that comes from being blamed as a trouble-maker, there is also guilt associated with being too healthy or successful, or with becoming your own person.

Engel and Ferguson (1990) state that some people feel guilt for "imaginary crimes." In their view, there are a few different types of imaginary crimes that are actually the result of healthy choices we make in our lives.

The first of these imaginary crimes is referred to as "outdoing," and it consists of excelling in life so that you surpass other family members. Thus, you may feel guilty of the crime of outdoing a family member simply by being happier or more successful than they are. A man named Harry provides us with a good example of guilt brought on by his perception that he was outdoing his father.

Harry's father had always had the dream of being a successful entrepreneur, and he had participated in a number of unsuccessful "get-rich-quick" schemes. For as long as Harry could remember, his father would say that he was right on the brink of the ultimate money-making success. Harry looked up to his father, and decided that when he grew up, he would try to be just like him.

When he finished college, he started a software engineering business, following his father's entrepreneurial spirit. Within five years, his business had grown from a one-man-show to a large corporation with hundreds of employees. Harry was surprised, however, that the bigger his business became, the more ill at ease he felt.

He began to dread hearing profit reports, because the more money he made, the more guilt he felt that he was "too successful." He felt completely unable to enjoy his success, because he worried he was betraying his father by surpassing him in the thing his father loved best, business. Harry was locked up in the imaginary crime of outdoing.

Another of these crimes is called "love theft," and it involves feeling that you received love and attention from your parents that your brother or sister needed in order to grow into a healthy person.

Susan can remember always being her parents' favorite child, and her little brother Ricky was always considered the "pain in the neck." She enjoyed the consistent attention of her parents, as they consistently attended her piano recitals and praised her for her good grades.

However, Susan often felt bad that Ricky rarely received praise for anything he did. Mom and Dad just tried to ignore Ricky whenever possible. Even when he did something good, somehow Mom and Dad didn't seem to notice like they did when Susan accomplished good things.

Ricky had numerous behavior problems throughout his school years and ended up dropping out of high school.

As an adult, Susan didn't talk to Ricky much, because she felt unbearable guilt about how differently her parents had treated the two of them when they were growing up. This guilt stood as a barrier between her brother and herself, and they weren't able to have a close relationship. Susan felt that she had somehow stolen the parental love that Ricky needed to thrive.

Two other types of imaginary crimes are abandonment and disloyalty. In abandonment, we may decide to take the healthy step of separating from our parents by moving away when we go to college or get married. We feel that by doing this we are taking away our parents' reason for living.

By developing separate lives, we may feel that we are leaving our parents behind without their primary focus in their lives, which was once taking care of us.

Another "imaginary crime," disloyalty, involves the guilt we feel when we criticize our parents or when the choices we make fail to meet their standards or expectations.

When we decide to go our own way in terms of partner or career choice and we go against values our parents may have tried to teach us, we may suffer from guilt arising from feeling disloyal.

How many of us feel guilty that we are not living up to our parent's expectations in one way or another?

ACTIVITY 4:

IDENTIFYING GUILT-INDUCING FAMILY BEHAVIORS

Identifying the different behaviors in your family of origin is important in understanding your feelings of shame and guilt. Which family behaviors have you noticed in your family of origin and within yourself? Check all that apply.

- ❐ Blaming
- ❐ Scapegoat
- ❐ Disloyalty
- ❐ Abandonment
- ❐ Love theft
- ❐ Outdoing
- ❐ Perfectionistic standards
- ❐ Other

Write down which roles different family members played in these behaviors.

What roles did you play in the dynamics of
your family of origin?

Explain how you still play those roles, or how
you still act out those family dynamics today,
either with family members or with significant
others in your life.

Conclusion

It is clear, then, that shame and guilt can come from a variety of different circumstances and experiences within our culture and family structure, many of which were beyond our control when we were growing up.

Our experiences with cultural attitudes and with our families of origin have formed us into who we are today. If we are to understand who we are and how shame and guilt affect our lives, we must continue to explore the roots of these emotions so that we will be able to identify and eventually change these excessive feelings of shame and guilt.

PART 3:

OVERCOMING UNHEALTHY SHAME AND GUILT

CHAPTER **4**

THE MIND/BODY/FEELING/ACTION APPROACH TO SHAME AND GUILT

Learning The Mind/Body/Feeling/Action Approach

Our Interactive Nature

The Mind/Body/Feeling/Action approach helps us to understand how shame and guilt function and how they are expressed in our thinking, our body, our feelings and our actions.

A major point of this approach is that our thoughts, our bodies, our feelings and our actions all affect one another as parts of the same system. In other words, each part affects all of the other parts.

For example, if you are having anxious feelings, your body may respond with butterflies in the stomach.

Given that all four parts of the Mind/Body/Feeling/ Action system affect one another, if we simply change one part of the system, then the other three parts will begin to shift as well.

For instance, changing our ways of thinking can ulti- mately change whether we feel shame or guilt, what our body sensations are, and our actions.

This diagram illustrates the interactive nature of our mind, body, feelings, and actions:

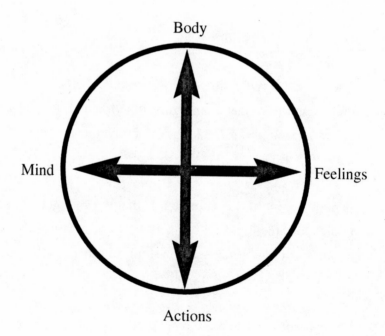

Here is an example to illustrate how our thoughts, feelings, body sensations, and actions are related to each other. Rita works at a bank. She finds out that her good friend Dan, a coworker at the bank, has been leaving work early but still indicating that he was at work on his time card.

She feels very angry with him, and feels that he has been dishonest with her, as well as with the bank. Besides the fact that he gets paid for hours he doesn't work, she also resents the fact that sometimes his leaving early has created more work for her.

She pulls Dan aside to talk to him about this matter. She brings up the subject with him, explaining what she knows, and intending to express her feelings about the situation.

Dan does not react well, and immediately becomes highly defensive and angry.

The next thing Rita knows, she finds herself standing there silently, shrinking in the corner of the office, being lectured by Dan about minding her own business.

She feels guilty, as if she were being reprimanded for something she has done wrong.

To her dismay he tells her that she is a terrible friend for not understanding this situation, and he cuts off his friendship with her. She feels bad and wonders what she did wrong.

She thinks about other times when her friendships haven't gone well, and feels that there must be something wrong with her. She feels shame. "I always screw up my friendships," she decides. "I am simply unable to keep friendships."

Rita feels deeply ashamed of herself, and withdraws from other friends, and family members. Her heart pounds out of intense fear, because she is certain that she will end up all alone in life. She imagines a future of isolation.

When she wakes up the next morning, she has a throbbing headache, and she calls in sick in order to avoid Dan and recuperate from the ordeal.

If we look at the different parts of the mind/body/feeling/action approach for Rita, we see that her mind is thinking, "I always screw up friendships." Her feelings are those of both shame and guilt. Her body responds with a pounding heart and a throbbing headache. Her actions are those of standing in the corner silently and calling in sick the next day.

It is clear in this vignette that Rita's thought that "I always screw up my friendships," leads her to feel both shame and guilt.

Her body is a part of this interactive loop that includes thoughts, feelings of shame and guilt, and now, a headache and a racing heart. Rita's body reactions, feelings, and thoughts in turn influence her actions of standing silently in the corner and calling in sick.

As Rita is overwhelmed by feelings of shame and guilt, and is thinking about the situation in a self-blaming way, she is not likely to take action to resolve the situation in a way that will be healthy for her.

In turn, if she watches her own passive reactions, they may confirm to her that indeed she should feel guilty, and that she is in the wrong.

As you can see, all of the parts in this system ultimately affect one another. Our mind, feelings, actions and body responses are all interrelated parts of the same system.

In the next sections, we take a closer look at the different parts of the mind/body/feelings/actions system.

The Mind

When we refer to the mind, we are really talking about our thoughts. Because our thoughts flow automatically through our minds all day and all night long, and we sometimes are not even aware of them, they are sometimes called automatic thoughts.

For most of us, we are so busy completing the tasks of the day that we never turn our attention to what we are thinking. If we did turn our attention to our thoughts and listen to them, we would discover all sorts of thinking patterns we never realized existed.

These thinking patterns have become habits for us, because we have thought in these ways for many years. We use these thinking patterns to interpret most of the situations in which we find ourselves.

For example, after Rita received the angry response from Dan at the bank, her thinking patterns determined how she interpreted the situation. She blamed herself for everything that happened between herself and Dan, and because of this thinking pattern, she felt ashamed, guilty, and extremely upset about her ability to maintain friendships.

There are however, a number of other ways in which she could have looked at this incident. She could have focused on Dan's actions instead, saying to herself, "I can't believe that he is trying to defend his actions when he is so clearly wrong. Then he tries to make me feel bad because I have some feelings about him leaving early and creating more work for me. It doesn't seem like his friendship is any great loss!"

If we pay attention to our thinking patterns, they can give us clues about how we get stuck in the same ways of interpreting events around us. The even better news is that if we begin to pay attention to our habitual ways of thinking, we can actually start to change them. We can retrain ourselves to not always blame ourselves (feel guilty), and to not always look to ourselves to see "what is wrong with us" (feel shame).

Automatic thoughts have been programmed into our minds through hearing them from others over many years. If you have heard a parent or some other person tell you repeatedly that you are stupid, you will start to believe that it is true, whether or not it has any basis in fact whatsoever.

Think about the kinds of statements about yourself that you heard from parents while you were growing up. Some examples of statements people hear are: "You're just a stupid girl" or "you're a sissy" or "you never do anything right" or "nobody likes you" or "you are such a pain in the neck" or "you're going to give me a heart attack!"

When we hear these kinds of shame or guilt-inducing statements about ourselves over and over again, and they become associated with experiences of rejection, they have a profound impact on our beliefs about ourselves. They begin to seem true to us, even though they have only been said because the person who said them is irritable, or depressed, or very critical.

As children, we don't realize that these statements actually tell us more about the person who said them than about the person to whom they refer.

Later, when we have been programmed with these negative thoughts about ourselves, we use these thoughts to interpret our everyday experiences.

When a particular situation arises, we don't even have to think about how to interpret the situation. These thoughts arise automatically to "help" us interpret events.

Automatic thoughts are often distorted or untrue. For example, Tim heard his mother say hundreds of times as a child, "You are stupid and worthless." Now, whenever Tim is in a new situation and feeling a little unsure of himself, he automatically hears the thought in the back of his mind, "I am stupid and worthless."

ACTIVITY 1:

IDENTIFYING AUTOMATIC THOUGHTS

Can you identify any distorted automatic thoughts that come to mind in particular situations? List three distorted automatic thoughts that seem to arise whenever you try to interpret particular situations.

Where did these thoughts come from? Can you remember particular people in your life, either as a child or as an adult, who have ever said these particular distorted statements to you? List those people here.

What specifically did these people say to you which has contributed to developing these distorted automatic thoughts?

From these exercises, you can start to develop a general idea of some of the automatic thoughts or messages which you use to help interpret situations that arise.

Distortions in Thinking

Distorted thinking patterns have certain characteristics in common. Knowing some of these identifying characteristics can help you to determine when you are in the grip of an automatic thought that is distorting your perception of a situation. The first step in changing your automatic thoughts is to become aware of how they work.

There are several well-known distortions in thinking (also known as cognitive distortions) which are thought to underlie faulty and psychologically unhealthy interpretations of events. Some of the cognitive distortions which could be relevant to shame and guilt are presented here.

Blaming is a distorted thought pattern in which we believe that someone needs to be blamed for any bad things that happen. You may blame yourself or someone else. Remembering Rita from an earlier vignette, Rita chose to blame herself for the friendship with Dan ending. She could have blamed Dan, or she could have blamed both herself and Dan, or no one at all, thinking they just were not a good fit for friendship. The cognitive distortion here is that she chose to blame someone, and the fact that she chose to blame herself caused her to have guilt feelings.

All-or-nothing thinking occurs when you view the world in terms of absolute polarities or extremes. An event or situation is viewed as either all black or all white, all good or all bad. There is no middle ground; there are only extremes. In the vignette, Rita felt as though, "I always screw up my friendships." There is no middle ground here.

Another kind of thought distortion, *filtering,* refers to focusing on one part of a situation, basing your conclusions on that one part and filtering out all of the other parts that would contradict that conclusion. Here is an example of filtering. John gives a presentation to a class. During the presentation, he drops one of the posters he is using for his presentation. At the end of the presentation, he receives enthusiastic applause.

However, John's thoughts run like this: "Oh my God, I am such an idiot. I am so embarrassed that I dropped that poster. I must have looked so ridiculous. I'm no good at doing presentations." John's exclusive focus on his poster mishap keeps him from noticing the applause which shows that the audience enjoyed his presentation. He filters out all of the perceptions that the members of his class were very impressed, and that he actually has a gift for presenting. The only perception that is allowed through the filter is the moment that the poster dropped. His narrow thinking about his one mistake leads him into a deep well of shame.

If John were able to stop filtering out all of the positive feedback he received and instead focus on the applause he received for his presentation, he could then avoid feelings of shame and enjoy feelings of pride instead.

Overgeneralization is a distorted thinking pattern that involves taking one event (usually a negative one) and generalizing your conclusions about that event to other areas of your life.

For instance, if a family member told you that you had hurt her feelings, you might assume that you are hurting people's feelings in all other areas of your life, such as family relationships or at work. The distorted thought might go something like this: "I just can't get along well with other people and I never have."

Mind reading refers to making conclusions about what someone else is thinking without checking out the accuracy of your conclusions with the other person. The automatic thoughts that cause shame or guilt are often based on faulty assumptions that other people think negatively of us.

In reality, if we ask others what they think of us, they may not be thinking negatively towards us at all. We may jump to conclusions without getting more information to help prove or disprove our own assumptions.

Catastrophizing involves interpreting difficult situations as absolutely devastating events from which there will be no hope of recovery. For example, if Rita came to the conclusion that "her whole life was over" because her friendship with Dan was over, this would be an example of catastrophizing.

Another cognitive distortion, *personalization,* occurs when you interpret all events around you in terms of yourself and your self-worth. This type of thinking would actually be helpful if you were to attribute good things which occur to your great personality.

However, most people who experience excessive shame and guilt tend to personalize only negative experiences as proof of their shortcomings or of their defectiveness as a human being.

Emotional reasoning involves interpreting a situation solely based on your feelings. " I feel guilty, therefore I am guilty." For those who feel excessive guilt, emotional reasoning can be a truly overwhelming enemy. Based on emotional reasoning, the guilt-based person will assume responsibility and blame for nearly every negative event which occurs.

A related type of cognitive distortion is the belief that you
need to follow an indisputable, rigid set of rules which
are usually expressed as *"shoulds," "shouldn'ts,"*
"musts," "oughts" or *"have-tos."*

For example, some of us feel that in every situation,
there is a right or wrong thing to do (a "should"),
rather than a more flexible response. If we have failed
to figure out what we "should" do in a set of circumstances, we feel lost. If we have failed to accomplish
what we have determined we "should" do, we are
filled with guilt and self-criticism.

The problem with thinking in "shoulds" and "oughts"
is that oftentimes, there are several courses of action
which could be equally appropriate. We may be preoc-
cupied with trying to find the one "right" course of
action we "should" take, when there are actually a
number of alternatives.

Another problem with "shoulds" is that often what we
think is the "right" way is simply the way that would
please others. It might not be the most healthy course
of action for ourselves. In order to explore the types of
distorted thinking that lead you to feel shame or guilt,
participate in the next activity.

ACTIVITY 2: IDENTIFYING DIFFERENT KINDS OF AUTOMATIC THOUGHTS

Check off any of the automatic thoughts that you currently have.

- ❐ Blaming
- ❐ All-or-nothing thinking
- ❐ Filtering
- ❐ Overgeneralization
- ❐ Mind reading
- ❐ Catastrophizing
- ❐ Personalizatin
- ❐ Emotional reasoning
- ❐ Other

What kinds of distortions do you notice in your automatic thoughts?

Do any of these distorted thoughts lead you to
feel shame? Look for key words and ideas in
your automatic thoughts which suggest shame
themes. For example, shame-inducing thoughts
usually have a lot of harsh criticism about some
quality you supposedly have, or something
being defective about you.

Identify any patterns in your thinking that contain this type of material.

How about guilt-inducing material? In your automatic thoughts, do you find any elements that would lead to guilt feelings? Guilt-inducing thoughts usually contain harsh criticism of something you did for which you will never be forgiven. Usually there is no possibility of forgiveness or pardon in the future, because the action you have done is seen as unpardonable. Other guilt themes might center around criticizing yourself for not taking care of things that you feel you "should" have taken care of. Look for "should" statements.

Identify any patterns in your thinking that contain this type of material.

Using this list of distorted thinking patterns can help you to become aware of your own particular set of thinking patterns. Your body's responses can also be a clue to help you detect when you are experiencing excessive shame and guilt. In the next section, bodily manifestations of shame and guilt will be explored.

The Body

When we are are having shame or guilt thinking patterns, our body responds as well. The type of body sensations we have will be determined by our thoughts, feelings and actions. Think about the last time you felt intense guilt or shame. It's a sure bet that you did not just sit there calmly and peacefully as you experienced these emotions. You probably felt tension in your back or neck muscles, or a headache, or a churning in your stomach. You may even have felt panicky sensations like your heart pounding, or sweaty palms.

Shame and guilt are emotions that assault our sense of well-being. They come upon us in a storm, and we feel agitated, and defensive, self-critical and broken inside. They can threaten us down to the core of our being. Often shame and guilt will trap us into an inner debate about whether or not we have done something wrong or whether it's really true that something is fundamentally bad about us. We may find ourselves playing judge and jury with our very selves on trial. During all of this mental activity, our bodies get revved up for a fight. Any time our minds perceive a threatening situation, our bodies respond by getting us ready to defend ourselves. The amazing thing about the connection between the mind and body is that mental events alone can trigger our bodies into an arousal reaction. That is, all we have to do is think about an intensely shame or guilt-inducing situation, and our bodies begin to prepare for it. In the next section, you will learn exactly how the body prepares for threatening events in our lives.

The Fight-or-flight Response

You are walking across the street, and suddenly you see a car coming directly towards you at 50 miles per hour. Instantly, your body reacts. Within seconds, your adrenal glands flood your body with adrenaline. Your heart rate suddenly soars, you breathe more quickly, your muscles tense, your senses become extra focused, and you begin to sweat. You run as fast as you can to safety, out of the way of the oncoming car. You watch it pass in a flash, still going 50 miles per hour. You have just had a fight-or-flight reaction, and it saved your life.

Now imagine if we did not have this type of reaction available to us. All of the body systems that we need to protect ourselves might not respond, and we might not survive walking across the street that day. We would not have that extra efficiency of the heart and the lungs and muscular system to get us across that street fast!

The fight-or-flight response got its name from the two options we have in survival types of situations. That is, we can either stay and fight, or our other option is flight – fleeing the scene as quickly as possible. Both of these responses require extreme physical resources, and our bodies prepare us for intense exertion that happens within seconds to get us out of danger. The major problem with the fight-or-flight response is that in our fast-paced society, we get into the habit of having it turned on constantly.

We are in such a hurry most of the time that we become entirely accustomed to having our hearts pounding and our muscles tensed continuously for days, weeks, months, and even years on end. Any of you who suffer from frequent headaches, backaches, insomnia, or stomach pain may be running yourself at top speed every day. Likewise, if you find yourself getting sick with colds or flu often, these aches, pains and illnesses are signs that your body is crying out for you to stop, or at least to slow down.

If you consider the engine of a car, what happens when you drive your car many miles at top speeds? You put a strain on your engine; you run out of gas sooner, and your car begins to break down more frequently. We usually call this "wear and tear" on our cars, but do we stop to consider how treating our bodies this way can lead to "wear and tear" as well?

We are usually aware when we are putting a strain on our automobiles by driving them too hard. When a car overheats from overuse, a warning light comes on to tell us that the car needs some attention and care. Our bodies also have warning systems, and body pains such as headaches, stomachaches, and backaches are signals to us that our bodies are under strain. Unfortunately, because our society emphasizes and values speed, there are cultural pressures for us to move very quickly and maintain a high level of body stress and tension. Because of these pressures, we may ignore these warning signals.

Aside from body pains we may experience, there are other signals that tell us when our fight/flight system is activated. These fight-or-flight signals can run the gamut from a racing heart, quick and shallow breathing, dry mouth, muscular tension, diarrhea and stomach pain, to migraine headaches. We can begin to develop an awareness of whether or not we are in a prolonged fight-or-flight response, and use that information to change our behavior.

For example, when you feel your heart pounding, you can stop what you are doing, and engage in some relaxing activity to try to bring your body into a calmer state. In order to help you experience the powerful connection between your thinking and the fight-or-flight system, try the next activity,

ACTIVITY 3:

THE CONNECTION BETWEEN THOUGHTS AND THE FIGHT-OR-FLIGHT RESPONSE

You will need a watch with a second hand to take your pulse. First sit down and make yourself comfortable. Now take your pulse using the fingers of one hand on the wrist of the other hand. Don't use your thumb, because it has a pulse of its own. Either count the beats of your pulse for one whole minute, or count the beats for a half minute and then multiply the number by two. Write down your pulse rate,

Now imagine the last time you had a really intense episode of shame. Remember exactly how you felt physically at the peak of the shame feelings. Focus on the words of your thoughts. Hold that memory in your mind for one minute. Now take your pulse again, and write down your pulse rate.

Did your pulse rate go up from the first time to the second?

For many people, even thinking about an intense experience will get their bodies activated in a fight-or-flight response.

Usually our body responses to thoughts about an experience will be less intense than they would be to the actual experience. However, as this activity demonstrates, thoughts alone can be powerful in awakening our fight-or-flight system.

Another purpose of this activity is to determine whether you tend to have strong body arousal responses to experiences of shame.

If you found that your pulse rate did go up from merely thinking about a shame experience, you may want to focus your attention on the section of this chapter on changing body responses.

Shame and Guilt and the Fight-or-Flight Response of the Body

How are shame and guilt related to the fight-or-flight response?

Essentially, shame and guilt experiences seem threatening, because they call into question either the worthiness of your fundamental being, or of something you have done.

When you are in the midst of an intense shame or guilt experience, you may have terrifying fears of being punished or humiliated. It is no surprise that these fears can lead to extreme stress on your body.

Intense experiences of shame or guilt can trigger physical responses that resemble anxiety or panic, including a racing heart, shallow breathing, sweating, dry mouth, muscle tension, increased stomach acidity, and even bowel discomfort.

Intense self-doubt and worry accompany experiences of shame and guilt, and thoughts of this type get the body revved up for a fight.

ACTIVITY 4:
IDENTIFYING BODY RESPONSES
TO SHAME OR GUILT

Recalling a particular situation in which you were feeling intense shame or guilt, how did your body respond? Check all that apply.

☐ Stomach pain
☐ Headache
☐ Backache
☐ Neck ache
☐ Shoulder ache
☐ Shortness of breath
☐ Nausea
☐ Dizziness
☐ Heart racing
☐ Sweaty hands
☐ Diarrhea
☐ Fever
☐ Muscle tension
☐ Dry mouth
☐ Heat sensations in your face
☐ Other

Frequency: How Often Does Your Body Respond?

In the last week, how often were your feelings of shame or guilt accompanied by some of the physical signs listed above?

❐ Not once   ❐ Once

❐ A few times   ❐ Several times

❐ Every day   ❐ Several times a day

If you answered that your body responded to shame or guilt a few times or more during the past week, your excessive shame and/or guilt are very likely to be putting a strain on your body.

Summary

The severity of your body responses to shame or guilt is reflected in how often and how long your body responds to shame and guilt.

Look over your responses to the activities above, and you will get an idea of the extent of your body responses to shame and guilt. By examining the extent of our body responses, we have another signal as to whether we have excessive shame and/ or guilt.

Feelings

There are many different feelings which you can experience, such as happiness, sadness, depression, elation, guilt, shame, frustration, and anger. The first step in dealing with these emotions is to identify what you are feeling.

For some of us, this is not as easy as it sounds. Certain cultural groups are more emotionally expressive than others, and even within cultures, families vary in terms of how acceptable it is to experience and express emotions.

If you come from a cultural group and/or family in which it was not acceptable to share feelings with others, you may have particular difficulty knowing what you're feeling. If you think about it, this difficulty makes perfect sense. Growing up in an expressive type of family, when someone was sad, you would see the signs of it on their faces, and you would hear the word "sad."

If, on the other hand, you grew up in a family in which feelings were not very welcome, you would not have any examples to work with to help you recognize feelings in yourself or in others. You might even wonder if there was something wrong with you when you had a strong feeling.

Fortunately, identifying feelings is something you can learn. Working with a skilled therapist or with a supportive friend to talk about your reactions to situations can help you to begin to develop a "feeling vocabulary."

In terms of dealing with shame or guilt, being able to identify these feelings is essential. You must practice becoming aware of these emotions while they're happening in order to make use of the shame and guilt reducing techniques explained in this book.

ACTIVITY 5:

HOW WERE FEELINGS EXPRESSED

IN YOUR FAMILY?

What behavior did members of your family exhibit that would indicate they were having feelings?

- ☐ Yelling
- ☐ Crying
- ☐ Throwing things
- ☐ Withdrawing from others
- ☐ Being silent
- ☐ Talking about feelings
- ☐ Drinking alcohol
- ☐ Slamming doors
- ☐ Leaving the house
- ☐ Hitting someone
- ☐ Talking to oneself
- ☐ Eating excessively
- ☐ Taking drugs
- ☐ Excessive cleaning
- ☐ Hurting oneself
- ☐ Other

What feelings were expressed?

☐ Anger

☐ Sadness

☐ Guilt

☐ Embarrassment

☐ Hopelessness

☐ Frustration

☐ Tension

☐ Shame

☐ Happiness

☐ Exhilaration

☐ Loneliness

☐ Bitterness

☐ Irritability

☐ Cheerfulness

☐ Excitement

☐ Anxiety

☐ Hopefulness

☐ Other

What feelings were you comfortable expressing
in front of family members as you were growing up? How about now?

What feelings were very uncomfortable for you
to express in front of family members when
you were a child? How about now?

Do you have any specific memories of feeling
shame or guilt when you were growing up?
And now?

These activities should help you begin to develop an understanding of how aware you are of your feelings, and how that awareness has been shaped by your experiences in your family of origin. The activities should also help you get a sense of which feelings were acceptable in your family of origin, and which ones were not.

Actions

The action part of the system consists of your behavior in any given situation. Referring back to the vignette with Rita, when Rita received the negative, defensive response from Dan upon confronting him about his time card, her response was to stand there silently, shrinking into the corner. Unfortunately, her silence only served to reinforce her sense of having done something wrong that deserved Dan's punishing response. Had Rita stood in the same spot with her head held high and calmly explained to Dan again her objections to his behavior, she would have reinforced her own sense of personal power and self-respect.

Thus, our actions affect our thoughts and feelings, and vice versa. That is, if we act guilty, we are more likely to feel guilty, and even to think we are guilty. Of course, when Rita thought that she had done something wrong, her body responded as well, with a headache. As you can see, all four parts of the mind/body/feelings/action system affect one another.

How To Change Parts Of the System

Now you may be thinking, "All right, I understand the parts of the Mind/Body/ Feelings/Actions system and how they are interrelated, but how can I change them? How can I get rid of shame or guilt?" As mentioned previously, changing any one part in the system will affect all of the other parts.

The strategies presented next are only a few examples of the ways in which you can work with and change your responses to the world around you and within you.

We encourage you to be creative in developing ways that work especially well for you.

Changing Distorted Thinking Patterns

Suppose you find yourself in a very emotionally upsetting situation, and you have determined that you are experiencing strong feelings of guilt. How can you change those feelings?

With the ultimate aim of eliminating guilt feelings, let us start with the mind (thoughts) part. The first step is to identify any automatic thoughts you are having about the situation.

In order to do this, you need to tune in to what you are thinking. Recording your automatic thoughts is a technique that is frequently used in psychotherapy to help people become aware of the thinking patterns that lead them to feel the way they do.

We recommend that you keep a "thought record" for at least a week's time, and consistently write down your thoughts at regular intervals, such as every hour or every morning, afternoon and evening. Through this process, you will begin to notice patterns in your thinking. There may be certain thoughts which arise over and over again, and you may not have been aware of them before.

By the end of a week's time of recording your automatic thoughts, you should be able to identify the top two or three thoughts that have occurred most frequently. Once you have done this, congratulate yourself. You have just uncovered some of the most powerful motivators that drive the way you feel and behave in a number of situations!

In order to facilitate this process, you can use the next activity as a model of a thought record. Since it is also helpful to notice what you were feeling while having an automatic thought, a space is provided for recording feelings, too. You might want to continue your thought record in your journal.

ACTIVITY 6:
RECORDING YOUR AUTOMATIC THOUGHTS FOR A WEEK

Day   Date

Automatic Thought

Feelings While Having the Automatic Thought

Example:

Day   Date
Tuesday   August 21

Automatic Thought:
I should spend more time with my children.

Feelings While Having the Automatic Thought:
Guilty, sad, regretful, anxious.

The second step you need to take is to argue with these distorted or automatic thoughts. Let's look at an example.

Remember John, the young man who filtered out all evidence of his success and concluded that he wasn't any good at doing presentations? How could he begin to argue with this type of automatic thought?

An argument against his thought filtering might sound something like this: "It's not true that I do a lousy job at presentations. I have gotten good feedback from people in the past about my presentation skills, and even though I did make a mistake, everyone applauded me enthusiastically at the end."

How do defense attorneys build arguments to disprove something? They sift through evidence that disconfirms what their opponent has said.

Thus, building an argument to defend yourself against automatic thoughts involves sifting through evidence that contradicts your automatic thought.

After constructing the argument, you can use it to protect yourself against the automatic thought every time it presents itself. Gradually, with much practice, the argument process begins to chip away at the credibility of that automatic thought, and it no longer has such a hold on you.

Most people find that distorted thoughts die hard. They are very resistant to change, so John might have to argue against this automatic thought about his ability to do presentations hundreds of times.

Automatic thoughts become a part of our minds from hearing them from others hundreds of times. Therefore, it's going to take some substantial arguing to discredit these automatic thoughts.

Patience is the key, along with repetition. Just as a teacher must repeatedly correct students in order to help them learn, you must repeatedly correct your own thinking patterns.

New and healthy thinking patterns are habits that must be developed through continued practice.

To practice arguing against your automatic thoughts, try the next activity.

ACTIVITY 7:
ARGUING AGAINST
YOUR AUTOMATIC THOUGHTS

Day   Date

Automatic Thought

Argument Against the Automatic Thought

Example:

Day   Date
Wednesday   August 22

Automatic Thought:
I should spend more time with my children.

Argument Against the Automatic Thought:
It is the quality, not the quantity of time spent
with my children that counts. My children really know that I care about them.

Changing Body Responses

As mentioned earlier, we are all equipped with a fight-or-flight response system, and this system can become overly active when we are feeling threatened by intense shame or guilt.

The bad news, then, is that if you tend to have a lot of experiences of shame or guilt, you're likely to experience a number of stress-related symptoms like headaches, stomachaches, insomnia, and others.

The good news is that the body also has a relaxation response system as a check and balance to the fight-or-flight system.

The even better news is that we can do specific things to help activate the relaxation response system.

There are several ways of changing our shame and guilt-related physical responses. These approaches include relaxation techniques, meditation, deep breathing and massage, among others.

By setting aside time to tend to our body's needs for rest and relaxation, we interrupt the shaming and blaming messages that may be automatically going through our minds.

It is as though in relaxing, we are saying to our inner selves that all is well, and that no shame or guilt can threaten us.

Relaxation leads to feelings of deep well-being and a sense that all is well with the world.

To illustrate the usefulness of relaxation in counteracting guilty thoughts and feelings, let us look back to Rita. During her emotionally arousing encounter with her coworker, Rita could do some deep breathing to help her calm down, so she would not feel threatened by the condemning and guilt-inducing message he was directing at her. At lunch that day, Rita could be especially kind to herself by going to a quiet and nurturing place to relax.

By stimulating a relaxation response in her body, Rita is creating a body sensation that is not consistent with guilt feelings. Instead, her body sensations are consistent with feeling good about herself and her world.

Two of the most powerful methods of relaxation are deep breathing and visualization. We will describe these two basic techniques, and provide you with a couple of relaxation activities.

In our experience, it is useful to experiment with a variety of relaxation techniques in order to find the one that works the best for you. Fortunately, there are quite a few books available currently which can help you to learn more about the wide variety of ways to bring about the relaxation response.

Deep Breathing

Breathing is something we don't usually think about much. We are born knowing how to breathe deeply, using our bellies rather than our chests. If you watch a newborn sleep, you will see that with each breath, the newborn's belly will expand.

Unfortunately, most of us gradually begin to breathe using our chests as we grow into adulthood, and we may remain in that pattern for the rest of our adult lives. Thus, if you watch how an adult breathes, you will probably see that with each breath, his or her chest expands. Whereas the newborn is using the diaphragm to breathe, the adult is using the thorax or chest area.

Thoracic, or "chest breathing" can cause a lot of problems, because it unnecessarily activates the fight-or-flight response system.

When we are in a fight-or-flight response mode, we breathe shallowly, using our chests to help us breathe more quickly. Consequently, the body associates chest breathing with an emergency situation.

Each time we take a shallow breath using only the chest area, we are actually stimulating the nerves of the fight-or-flight response system and keeping it activated. When we breathe into the belly area instead, we stimulate our relaxation response system.

What this means is that calming ourselves down is completely within our control, by just changng our breathing pattern.

We can even slow down our heart rate, stop perspiration, lower our blood pressure, and decrease our muscle tension, thus activating the relaxation response instead of the fight-or-flight response, simply by changing our breathing patterns.

Deep breathing is the foundation of nearly every relaxation technique that exists. Nearly all of the relaxation techniques you can find will start with a direction to breathe more deeply and slowly.

Clearly, it is extremely important to teach yourself this relaxing breathing pattern. This exercise will teach you to use your diaphragm to breathe.

ACTIVITY 8:

LEARNING DIAPHRAGMATIC BREATHING

The key to this exercise is to learn to feel the difference between chest breathing and diaphragmatic breathing. For this exercise you will need a book, and a quiet place to lie down. Lie down on your back and make yourself comfortable. Place your right hand on your stomach, about the level of your navel. Place your left hand on your chest. Now pay attention to your breathing, and take a few deep breaths.

Notice which of your hands is rising and falling the most as you inhale and then exhale. The goal is to have the lower hand resting on your belly do most of the rising and falling, as you breathe in and out.

If the hand on your chest is rising and falling more than the one on your belly, you are breathing mostly into the chest area. Try to correct this by making the hand on your belly rise and fall as you inhale and exhale.

For some people, this exercise is very difficult, because they are unaccustomed to using the belly muscles to breathe.

If you find that you are having a hard time coordinating your muscles to breathe into the belly area, try using the book. Place it on your stomach. As you inhale, use your belly to push the book up. As you exhale, the book should go back down again.

As you continue to breathe diaphragmatically for several minutes, you will notice that relaxation begins to spread throughout your body. Eventually, you will begin to notice profound feelings of well-being, peace and calm. All of the fight-or-flight response systems have been turned off, and your deep breathing is a clear and continuing signal to your body that all is well and that you can relax.

Next you can try the visualization relaxation exercise below.

ACTIVITY 9:
VISUALIZATION EXERCISE

Lie down on your back and make yourself comfortable. Close your eyes and breathe deeply and slowly. After a few minutes of breathing deeply, focus your attention inward, and let go of any distracting thoughts.

Feel your arms, your legs, your body being supported beneath you. Just let the weight of your body rest on the floor.

Now mentally take yourself back to a place in which you felt very safe, very peaceful and calm. Imagine that place in detail – how it looked, what you smelled in the air, what it felt like. Just rest in that place for a while. Imagine your body in that place, feeling that place support your body as it rests. Continue to breathe deeply, breathing in the air of that place where you imagine yourself. As you inhale, notice your lungs taking in fresh air, and as you exhale, feel the old air leave your body.

Allow yourself to continue to breathe deeply and rest in this safe place for several minutes. When you are ready, begin to bring your awareness back to the present. Become aware of your breathing, and feel your abdomen rising and falling with each breath.

Open your eyes and slowly look around, as you become oriented to the room. Recognize and appreciate your feeling of peace and relaxation, and try to carry that with you throughout the rest of the day.

Changing Feelings

Working skillfully with your emotions can be a real challenge. However, there are some basic principles you can follow to learn to soothe, comfort and even modify how you are feeling.

The first step you can use when you are overwhelmed with feelings is to ask yourself what you need. Try to tune in to the part of yourself that feels agitated or vulnerable, and ask that part of you what would be soothing.

Comfort can come in many forms, including seeking the company of others, going to a safe, beautiful place, or deciding to have some fun, whatever fun means for you. The key element of this approach is simply to ask yourself what would make you feel better right now, and then do it.

Another basic principle in dealing with feelings is that simply expressing them can make them much more manageable. Feelings can build up within us and exert a kind of pressure that immediately decreases as soon as we begin to take them outside of ourselves by expressing them.

This pressure that we feel inside can be very frightening, and if we don't respond to our needs for expression, we can start to behave in self-destructive ways.

Expression of feelings can take many forms. Some people find it most helpful to express feelings verbally by talking with a supportive friend, therapist or loved one.

People who are more private may prefer to express feelings by writing in a journal. Still others may express themselves through art or music. Feelings may also be expressed in physical ways.

For example, if you are tired of feeling guilty and are maybe even a little angry about it, consider expressing that mixture of guilt and anger in a non-violent, physical way.

Some people go into their bedrooms and hit a pillow while thinking about what is making them feel guilty and angry. Nobody gets hurt, and this is an excellent way of freeing yourself from burdensome emotions.

If you find that your shame or guilt is mixed with sadness, crying might be a soothing activity. Crying releases a great deal of bodily tension, and leaves you relaxed and in a clearer state of mind.

Experiment with different ways of expressing yourself, and use the ones that feel the most natural to you.

ACTIVITY 10:

EXPRESSION OF FEELINGS

What are some of the ways you usually express your feelings? Rank each one from 1 to 5 according to how effective it is in helping you deal with feelings of shame or guilt.

What are some new ways you would like to try to express your feelings?

Changing Actions

There are a number of direct actions you can take which will diminish feelings of shame and guilt. The first step is to take an inventory of the situation that has provoked your feelings. What are the particulars of the situation, and who is involved in it? This examination process will help you to separate healthy shame or guilt from unhealthy, excessive shame or guilt. The course of action you decide to take will depend to some extent on whether the shame or guilt you are feeling is unhealthy or excessive.

As we explained in Chapter 1, sometimes when we feel shame or guilt, there is actually some action we could take to make the situation right, and taking this action would be the very best thing we could do to take care of ourselves. Perhaps there is someone we feel we have slighted, or some misjudgment we have made that has resulted in negative consequences for ourselves or other people. In that case, we can use a problem-solving approach to address the situation so that the best possible outcome can happen. In this type of situation, doing something really can make us feel better – less guilty, or less ashamed. The more difficult types of situations are those in which there really is nothing we can do to make things better. The healing from shame or guilt in these types of situations is much more lengthy. It requires the development of a deep compassion for yourself, and a humble understanding that as humans we are not perfect beings.

If you find through your examination that you are in a state of excessive, unhealthy shame or guilt, there are several ways to change these feelings. One of the most powerful concepts you can use to change a feeling such as shame or guilt is the idea that opposite moods are incompatible. If you put yourself in some situation in which it would be difficult to maintain feelings of guilt or shame, it is likely that these feelings will be reduced.

For example, if you come home feeling ashamed of yourself, and then you spend some time with a friend who greatly admires you and likes your company, it is very likely that your shame feelings will be reduced. You might even forget all about them. Suppose that you are feeling burdened by sadness and guilt. You might change the feeling watching a humorous film that makes you laugh. It is virtually impossible to remain in a depressed and self-critical emotional state while laughing.

When you find yourself in the middle of a guilt-inducing or shame-inducing situation, you can actually decide to change your behavior immediately and thus change your immediate feelings. Let's look at Rita again for an example of what not to do. Rita stood in the corner of Dan's office silently while he defended himself and tried to put the responsibility (blame) back on her. Her action of standing there silently in the corner contributed to her sensation of being reprimanded, as if she had actually done something wrong.

As a child, when you did something wrong in school, the teacher would reprimand you or lecture you while you stood there silently in the corner. Thus, repeating this pattern would probably reinforce the feeling of having done something wrong. In her passivity, she sends herself the message that she must have done something wrong. Why else would she be reacting this way if she was not guilty of misbehaving?

How could Rita have behaved differently so as to send herself a different message? She could have stood in the middle of the office, or at least not in the corner; she could have participated in the conversation instead of being silent; and she could have repeated her objections to Dan. If she confronted Dan yet again in this situation, she would be affirming to herself the appropriateness of confronting him the first time, rather than disconfirming it with her unassertive silent behavior.

The key is this: If you act guilty, you start to believe that you are. And if you do not act guilty, you will begin to realize you are actually free of guilt. Practice makes perfect. Changing your actions so that they are more consistent with how you would like to think and feel is very important.

ACTIVITY 11:
ACTIONS

What are the most helpful actions you take to
help you deal with feelings of shame and guilt?
Check all that apply.

- ❏ Taking a walk
- ❏ Lying down
- ❏ Reading a book
- ❏ Talking to a friend or loved one
- ❏ Getting exercise
- ❏ Journaling
- ❏ Painting or drawing
- ❏ Meditating
- ❏ Going to a movie
- ❏ Gardening
- ❏ Spending time in nature
- ❏ Working
- ❏ Taking a hot bath
- ❏ Hugging a stuffed animal
- ❏ Helping someone else
- ❏ Spending time with a pet
- ❏ Other

Think of a situation in which you felt shame or guilt. What were your actions?

Examine the situation and consider who was involved. What was your part in the situation?

Was your guilt or shame excessive and unhealthy?

After reading this last section, what actions would you take to reduce your feelings of shame or guilt?

Now that you have learned about all four parts of the Mind/Body/Feeling/Action approach to reducing shame and guilt, it is time to integrate all of these parts together.

When you are dealing with feelings of shame or guilt, it will be most helpful if you can use all four parts of the approach. In this way, you will have four different areas to target, and your chances of success are greatly increased.

ACTIVITY 12:
INTEGRATING THE FOUR PARTS OF THE MIND/BODY/FEELING/ACTION APPROACH

Think about an intense experience of shame or guilt you have had in your life. Using that experience as an example, what were your distorted automatic thoughts?

Do you remember any physical sensations that accompanied your experience of shame or guilt? If so, what were they?

What were your emotions in the situation? Aside from shame or guilt, did you experience other feelings such as embarrassment or tearfulness?

How did you behave in the shaming or guilt-inducing situation?

If you wanted to change your automatic thoughts, what arguments would you use against them?

How might these changes in automatic thinking affect you? Changes in your feelings:

Changes in your body sensations:

Changes in your actions:

How could you change your body responses to help reduce or eliminate your excessive shame or guilt?

How would changing body responses affect your thoughts?

How would changing body responses affect your feelings?

How would changing body responses affect your actions?

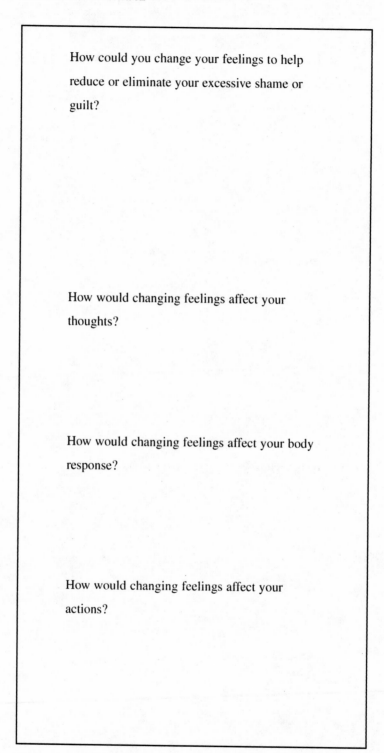

How could you change your feelings to help reduce or eliminate your excessive shame or guilt?

How would changing feelings affect your thoughts?

How would changing feelings affect your body response?

How would changing feelings affect your actions?

How could you change your actions to help reduce or eliminate your excessive shame or guilt?

How would changing actions affect your thoughts?

How would changing actions affect your body response?

How would changing actions affect your feelings?

CHAPTER 5

HEALING SHAME AND GUILT IN YOUR FAMILY OF ORIGIN

Circles of Relationships

You – From the Center Out

Since you have arrived at this chapter of the book, you have already learned about how shame and guilt enter our lives as children and continue to influence our interactions with others throughout our adulthood. As you think about your relationships with others, you can think of these relationships in terms of ever-widening circles. The innermost circle is you.

The second circle consists of your family-of-origin relationships, which will be covered in this chapter.

In the third circle are people with whom you have daily interaction, including significant others, friends, and possibly, coworkers and your superiors at work.

CIRCLES OF RELATIONSHIPS

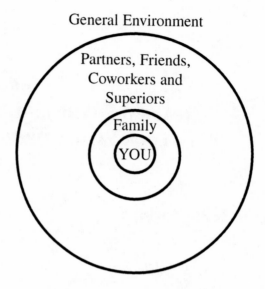

Outside of this circle is your general environment, which includes acquaintances whom you do not see often, strangers, and even bearers of societal messages such as the media.

As stated in Chapter Two, even though you may not interact actively with these influences, they still affect you, and may trigger unhealthy feelings of shame and guilt.

In Chapter Six you will learn how to reduce the shame and guilt you experience in the circles outside of your family of origin.

An Inventory of Shaming and Blaming Behaviors in Your Family of Origin

In the discussion of the mind/body/feeling/action approach in Chapter Four, you learned how to change your thoughts, feelings, actions, and body responses so as to lessen excessive feelings of shame and guilt. Now you can begin to apply what you have learned to specific interpersonal situations, beginning with your family.

Shame and guilt often originate from your family of origin, meaning the family in which you were raised. Therefore there is no better place to start to apply your new knowledge base than to improve your relationships within your family of origin.

Even if you do not have any current contact with your parents or other family members because they have passed away or live across the world, you still may hear their voices in your head continuing the episodes of shame and guilt. For example, even though Jane's mother died five years ago, she can still hear her mother telling her she is a failure every time she makes a mistake. Jane has internalized her mother's statements to her and now she says them to herself.

Many of us do have some contact with our families. There is much that we can do to reduce our family's current contribution to our shame and guilt. The first step in changing old patterns of behavior is awareness.

ACTIVITY 1: IDENTIFYING SHAMING AND BLAMING BEHAVIORS IN YOUR MOTHER

Can you identify any shaming or blaming (guilt inducing) behaviors performed by your mother in either the past or present? Check all that apply.

❐ Physical abuse

❐ Sexual abuse

❐ Alcohol abuse

❐ Threatening to abandon you

❐ Drug abuse

❐ Ignoring you

❐ Yelling at you

❐ Calling you negative names like "stupid," "bad," or "worthless"

❐ Making fun of you

❐ Making you take care of her when you were a child

❐ Fighting with you

❐ Talking down to you or patronizing you

❐ Making harmful statements such as "I don't love you" or "you don't deserve to exist"

❐ Other

ACTIVITY 2: IDENTIFYING
SHAMING AND BLAMING BEHAVIORS
IN YOUR FATHER

Can you identify any shaming or blaming (guilt inducing) behaviors performed by your father? Check all that apply.

❒   Physical abuse

❒   Sexual abuse

❒   Alcohol abuse

❒   Threatening to abandon you

❒   Drug abuse

❒   Ignoring you

❒   Yelling at you

❒   Calling you negative names like "stupid," "bad," or "worthless"

❒   Making fun of you

❒   Making you take care of him when you were a child

❒   Fighting with you

❒   Talking down to you or patronizing you

❒   Making harmful statements such as "I don't love you" or "you don't deserve to exist"

❒   Other

ACTIVITY 3: IDENTIFYING SHAMING AND BLAMING BEHAVIORS IN YOUR SIBLINGS

Can you identify any shaming or blaming (guilt inducing) behaviors performed by your sister/s or brother/s? Check all that apply.

☐ Physical abuse

☐ Sexual abuse

☐ Alcohol abuse

☐ Threatening to abandon you

☐ Drug abuse

☐ Ignoring you

☐ Yelling at you

☐ Calling you negative names like "stupid," "bad," or "worthless"

☐ Making fun of you

☐ Making you take care of them when you were a child

☐ Fighting with you

☐ Talking down to you or patronizing you

☐ Making harmful statements such as "I don't love you" or "you don't deserve to exist"

☐ Other

Becoming aware of behaviors from your family which sent you into a spiral of shame or guilt is the first step in learning how to ultimately change how you respond to family members.

We cannot really expect to change anyone but ourselves. Thus, focusing on how we want to respond differently to our family's shaming and blaming behaviors is the key.

There are four major ways we can change how we react and respond to these situations, and these involve changing our thoughts, body responses, feelings, and/or actions.

It is important to first identify the specific automatic thoughts which we have in relation to feelings of shame and guilt.

ACTIVITY 4: IDENTIFYING YOUR AUTOMATIC THOUGHTS

Every day for one week, on an hourly basis, keep track of what your thoughts are in situations in which you feel shame and guilt. Keep track of your thoughts by writing them in a journal as in the example below.

Day: Monday, August 21
9 AM - 10 AM
Situation: I made a mistake at work.
Thoughts: I'm an idiot because I made a mistake.

10 AM - 11 AM
Situation: I keep making mistakes at work.
Thoughts: I ought to just go home and forget it.

11 AM - Noon
Situation: Well, I got through the morning!
Thoughts: Maybe I can make it through the day anyway.

Noon - 1 PM
Situation: I forgot to tip the waitress at lunch.
Thoughts: Guilty. I'm afraid to go back to that restaurant.

This exercise was designed to help you monitor and identify your most common distorted automatic thoughts.

After you have taken at least a week or more to allow yourself to become aware of and identify your automatic thoughts, go on to the next exercise.

Upon becoming aware of the thoughts which you have in shaming and blaming situations, you will begin to notice some themes. The next exercise will help you identify and focus on the themes that are the most important to you.

ACTIVITY 5: IDENTIFYING THEMES IN YOUR AUTOMATIC THOUGHT RESPONSES

Here are a few examples of some automatic thoughts. Check all that apply, and add your own.

❐ I am a bad person.

❐ I am not worthy.

❐ I always screw up.

❐ I'll never be loved.

❐ I am so unworthy that my mother or father will never love me.

❐ I am so unworthy that my brother or sister will never love me.

❐ I am stupid.

❐ I don't deserve good things.

❐ I'm a horrible person.

❐ Other

ACTIVITY 6: IDENTIFYING
SOURCES OF SHAME AND GUILT

Now that you are aware of what kind of distorted automatic thoughts you have developed in relation to your family's past and present behavior, it is time to identify the sources of the thoughts and challenge them.

For each of your automatic thoughts, write down the source of those thoughts, or who you remember saying them to you in your family of origin. Then ask yourself if you believe it is acceptable to say them to your own child or anyone else.

Example:

Automatic Thought   **Who said that?**

I am unworthy.   Father

Would you say that to your own child

or anyone else?   No

Automatic Thought   **Who said that?**

Would you say that to your own child

or anyone else?

In this exercise, you identified the original sources of your distorted automatic thoughts that produce shame and guilt. By asking yourself whether you would treat anyone else that way, hopefully this will help you realize that it is never acceptable to treat anyone with such disrespect.

Now it is time to change those thoughts using some of the previously learned exercises. You are simply going to refute and challenge these distorted, negative thoughts and replace them with new positive thoughts.

ACTIVITY 7: CHALLENGING YOUR OLD AUTOMATIC THOUGHTS

What are some encouraging new thoughts that you can use to challenge your old automatic thoughts?

Example:

Old Thought

I am unworthy.

New Thought

I am worthy because I am kind to others.

Old Thought

I'm a bad person.

New Thought

I'm a good person
because I care
about others.

Old Thought

I do not deserve
to be loved.

New Thought

I deserve to be
loved as much
as anyone else.

Old Thought

New Thought

Old Thought

New Thought

Old Thought

New Thought

Old Thought

New Thought

Challenging your old thoughts and replacing them with new ones involves saying the new thought to yourself every single time the old thought pops into your mind. If you think about how many thousands of times you heard the old thoughts, deeply ingraining them into your mind, you can see that you are going to have to practice these new thoughts several times, as well.

These old automatic thoughts are merely habitual, meaning that you automatically think these thoughts out of habit. So, in order to break an old habit, you must repetitiously practice a new habit which will take the place of the old habit.

Just like when some smokers decide to quite smoking and they replace the old smoking behavior with chewing gum, you will be replacing old thoughts with new ones.

You are going to replace some very distorted automatic thoughts with some newer ones that fit much better.

Tips on How to Practice Challenging Old Automatic Thoughts

You may be saying to yourself, I know I need to practice these new thoughts thousands of times because these old ones are so deeply ingrained in my mind, but how do I do that exactly? Here are just a few tips to help make that happen. You may also think of your own ways of practicing your new thoughts that work well for you. Be creative.

✔ Write your new thoughts onto little slips of paper and post them someplace you are sure to see and read them daily, such as: the dash of the car, the bathroom mirror, the refrigerator door, the desk at work, the front door, the bedroom door, the computer monitor, or wherever you look frequently.

✔ Every time you see your new thoughts on your little slips of paper, read them three times at a glance.

✔ Say them out loud or to yourself, but say them.

✔ Even if you don't believe them, *SAY THEM ANY-WAY!*

✔ Remember how these automatic thoughts were created in the first place. Someone said them to you over and over, until eventually you internalized them and believed them.

✔ What you are doing now is undoing or relearning new thoughts. Believe it or not, eventually after hearing these new thoughts over and over, you will believe these new thoughts, as well.

✔ Say your new thoughts twenty times before you go to sleep.

✔ Write them in a journal every day.

✔ Even after you start believing your new thoughts/ beliefs, every now and then, refresh yourself by doing some of these tips again.

Identifying and Changing Body Responses

Being able to identify your body responses during episodes of shame or guilt can also aid in altering your feelings of shame and guilt.

If you can become aware of your body responses which are associated with guilt and shame, then you can learn how to alter those body responses and, ultimately, change your feelings of shame and guilt.

Consider Marsha, whose brother molested her when she was a young child. Marsha realizes now that she gets stomach aches at family gatherings when she is around her brother, and she falls into a deep spiral of shame.

In other words, her stomach ache signals to her that she is feeling excessive shame.

When Marsha reads that body signal, she has two choices of action to reduce her shame feelings.

She can choose to get rid of her stomach aches through relaxation, breathing, or meditation. Or, she can simply choose to remove herself from the situation by leaving the room. Either option leads to decreased stomach aches and shame feelings.

Our body responses are really signals that can help us to identify feelings of which we are not fully aware. It is important to learn to identify your body responses because sometimes it is difficult to distinguish whether you are feeling shame or guilt.

ACTIVITY 8: CHANGING YOUR BODY RESPONSES TO FAMILY MEMBERS

Remember a situation in your family of origin, either when you were a child or as an adult, in which you had some responses in your head, stomach, back, or other body system, in response to feelings of shame or guilt.

Check ideas from the list below of what you would choose for reducing and eliminating your body responses if you have them again.

- ❐ Take a meditation class.
- ❐ Do some deep breathing.
- ❐ Take a Yoga class.
- ❐ Take a Tai Chi class.
- ❐ Remove yourself from the stressful situation.
- ❐ Practice some of your new thoughts.
- ❐ Do some physical exercise.
- ❐ Others

Practice these techniques on a daily or as needed basis, especially when you are visiting your family of origin.

After you practice these techniques, your body responses may lessen over time. Ultimately you will have more tools to manage your feelings of shame and guilt.

For some people, knowing how they feel is an easy task. Yet for others, it may be a little more difficult to know what they are feeling, especially if they are accustomed to ignoring feelings or using substances like drugs or food to numb them. Use the next activity to become aware of and identify your feelings.

ACTIVITY 9: YOUR FAMILY'S SHAMING OR BLAMING BEHAVIORS

Remember a situation, either when you were a child or as an adult, in which a family member engaged in inappropriate shaming or blaming behaviors. How did it make you feel? Check all that apply.

☐ Happy ☐ Sad

☐ Worthless ☐ Helpless

☐ Ashamed ☐ Scared

☐ Guilty ☐ One inch tall

☐ Self-loathing ☐ Anxious

☐ Depressed ☐ Numb

Expressing, Releasing, and Giving Back Feelings

In the exercises above, you may have become aware of excessive feelings of guilt or shame. You have already taken the first step towards healing.

Next, you can talk about your feelings with a friend, sponsor, or therapist. Sometimes just talking about your feelings with someone else makes you feel better, because when you keep feelings bottled up inside of you, they will often leak out at inappropriate times.

If you do not feel like talking about your feelings with another person, you can express your feelings through art, music, journaling or writing the exercises like the ones in this book, or any other form of expression. The point is that once you express your feelings, then you can begin to release them.

If one of your parents or siblings caused you to feel shame or guilt as a child, then they are the rightful owners of that feeling.

You can choose to give them back that excess baggage if you no longer wish to claim it.

When you give back the shame or guilt to its rightful owner, you are making that individual take responsibility for her or his actions.

As an adult, no one can force you to feel shame or guilt. It is ultimately your choice whether you will accept the shame or guilt that someone has tried to give you.

You can choose how to respond to difficult family members.

Expressing, releasing, and giving feelings of shame and guilt back to the individuals who gave them to you in the first place are all major steps towards changing how you feel.

ACTIVITY 10: EXPRESSING AND RELEASING FEELINGS OF SHAME AND GUILT FROM YOUR FAMILY OF ORIGIN

Remember a situation in your family of origin, either as a child or as an adult, in which you felt excessive feelings of guilt or in which you were in a spiral of shame.

Check ideas from the list below that describe how you would like to express and release your feelings.

❏ Talking with that family member

❏ Writing/journaling

❏ Paint, art, sculpt, or other art forms

❏ Play/ listen to music

❏ Talk with a friend

❏ Talk with your sponsor

❏ Talk with your psychotherapist

❏ If sad, cry

❏ If angry, scream or hit a pillow

❏ Exercise

❏ Others

ACTIVITY 11: EXAMINE YOUR OWN BEHAVIORS AND ACTIONS IN RESPONSE TO YOUR FAMILY'S SHAMING OR BLAMING BEHAVIORS

Now that you are aware of how to change the automatic thoughts, body responses, and feelings you have in response to the shaming and blaming behavior in your family of origin, it is time to look at your own behavior.

Describe a situation in which a member of your family shamed or blamed you.

Remember, if you act guilty, then you start to feel that you are guilty. If you act ashamed, then you may start yourself down the spiral of shame.

Check all of the behaviors listed that apply.

When someone in my family engages in a shaming or blaming behavior, I tend to...

❐ Look down

❐ Shrink in the corner

❐ Agree with whatever is being said

❐ Become silent

❐ Stand there and just listen obediently

❐ Drink alcohol excessively

❐ Run away

❐ Do drugs excessively

❐ Eat excessively

❐ Cry

❐ Shop excessively

❐ Work excessively

❐ Harm myself physically, i.e. put my fist through a wall or cut on myself

❐ Harm others, i.e. hit someone else or kick the dog

❐ Go hide under the covers

❐ Other

Condoning and supporting shaming and blaming behaviors towards you.

Many of the responses listed above send the message that you have done something wrong or that you are a bad person. When someone in your family engages in a shaming or blaming behavior, and you stand there quietly, shrinking in the corner, you are giving that person and yourself the message that they are absolutely right, and you are wrong. All that are watching would be likely to assume that you did do something wrong if you are cowering quietly in the corner with a guilty look on your face. When we act guilty or shameful, we not only feel guilty and shameful but may appear that way to anyone else who is watching. In other words, when we act guilty and shameful, we are condoning and supporting that shaming and blaming behavior in our family.

Consider Maria, who used to stand there nodding silently, agreeing with her father when he would tell her that she was fat and ugly. She would drink alcohol and eat excessively so as to numb out her painful feelings of shame and guilt. As long as Maria continued to respond by just standing there, nodding silently, acting guilty and full of shame, her father's behavior was likely to continue. In fact, her inaction was condoning and supporting her father's actions of telling her she was fat and ugly. Whenever Maria did not confront her father's inappropriate statements, she was in effect saying , "You're right, I am fat and ugly, therefore you have every right to speak to me that way."

Additionally, when Maria would eat and drink alcohol excessively in reaction to her father's harsh words, she would gain weight, acting in just the way her father perceived her. When Maria would drink alcohol and eat excessively, she would not feel any pain. However, afterwards she would feel as if she had done something wrong. She would have tremendous guilt because she was gaining weight from her own actions.

How could Maria change her actions so as not to support and condone her father's behaviors and make her feel better about herself?

Confrontation, setting boundaries, and assertiveness.

Often in shame and guilt bound families, there are poorly-defined boundaries between family members. In these families, one member can tell another that she is fat and ugly, or anything else critical, for that matter. There are no accepted limits between members about what is or is not appropriate to say to one another.

If anyone ever says or does something to you that is demeaning, patronizing, and unacceptable to you, as a human being you have the right to just walk away.

What could Maria do differently in her situation with her father? She could confront him and set a boundary by saying, "I do not like it when you say I am fat and ugly. It is demeaning and patronizing, and makes me feel shameful about who I am as a person. I would appreciate it if you not only stopped saying that I am fat and ugly but if you halted all criticisms." Since her father might well respond by saying, "Screw you!" Maria could prepare herself beforehand for his negative response. She might say, "Dad, I want you to know that I will not be coming back into your house until you stop criticizing me and start treating me with respect."

When Maria's father is being disrespectful, Maria might simply walk away and leave the situation, giving the clear message that his behavior is inappropriate and unacceptable to her. This would be another form of asserting herself. Additionally, Maria could choose not to eat or drink alcohol excessively in response to her father's inappropriate behavior. Instead, she could call a friend, her sponsor, or her therapist to talk about it.

When Maria eats and drinks alcohol excessively, it ultimately makes her feel worse instead of better. Setting boundaries, confronting others, and limiting contact with some family members not only stops endorsing the inappropriate behavior, but is empowering to the victim as well.

Changing your own actions to make them more congruent with your new thoughts, body responses, and feelings will stabilize and strengthen these new aspects of you, and help get rid of the old thoughts, feelings, and body responses once and for all.

Confronting family members to set boundaries about unacceptable behavior involves being assertive. If you are not used to assertive behavior, it may take some time and practice to learn. When you are learning assertive behavior, it is sometimes easier to start small and work your way up to the more difficult levels of assertion.

For example, if you would like to eventually be able to tell your father to stop criticizing you or you will stop visiting him, you may want to start with some easier assertive behaviors first.

For many people, assertiveness with family members is more difficult than assertiveness with other people. In order to practice this new assertive behavior, you might first try telling your neighbor to stop knocking over your trash cans, or asking the newspaper boy not to throw your paper underneath your car.

When you practice easier assertive behavior, then you will be better prepared to perform more difficult assertive behavior.

ACTIVITY 12: YOUR NEW ACTIONS IN RESPONSE TO YOUR FAMILY'S SHAMING OR BLAMING BEHAVIORS

Check all that apply in this list, and think of others which apply to you.

❏ Don't look down, – make eye contact.

❏ Don't shrink in the corner – stand your ground.

❏ Don't just agree with whatever is being said – say how you feel.

❏ Don't be silent – speak your mind.

❏ Don't act obediently like a child being scolded – be an adult and assert yourself.

❏ Don't drink alcohol excessively – call a friend, sponsor, or therapist instead.

❏ Don't run away – stand your ground.

❏ Don't do drugs excessively – call a therapist instead.

❏ Don't eat excessively – call a friend instead.

❏ Don't shop excessively – call a sponsor instead.

❏ Don't work excessively – call a therapist instead.

❏ Don't harm yourself or anyone else – call a friend, sponsor, or therapist instead.

Now that you know which new behaviors and actions you need to do, it is time to start practicing them. Just as you practice your new improved thoughts, you must practice your new behaviors repetitiously and consistently for them to become your new habitual way of acting.

For example, this means for Maria that every time she speaks with her father, either in person, by telephone, or by letter, she will need to practice asserting herself, setting boundaries and limits.

This is no easy task at first. If you have never set boundaries or limits with family members before, it will take awhile to get the hang of it. It will feel awkward, foreign, and maybe even a little scary at first just because it is so new for you. But the good news is that it does get easier with time and practice.

It is important to pick your battles. You do not need to confront every person in your life over each little thing they do that bothers you.

It will be less tiring if you decide which are the important battles to confront and which are less important ones that do not matter as much.

Don't Drown in the Past

When you are going back through your childhood and remembering episodes of shame and guilt in your family of origin so as to learn how to change how you feel now, it is easy to get stuck in your past.

The purpose of these exercises is not to go back in time and stay there in perpetual frustration, but to go back just enough to explore how your past experiences have shaped you into the person you are today. There are relatively few families who engage in shaming or blaming behaviors all of the time. There are no "all bad" or "all good" families.

Therefore, as you remember some of the more unpleasant experiences in your family, take some time to remember some of the good times, as well.

This is a great time to remember some of the wonderful experiences you had within your family of origin and appreciate them.

ACTIVITY 13: REMEMBER SOME GOOD TIMES YOU HAD IN YOUR FAMILY

Take a moment to remember some of the good experiences you have had in your family of origin. Try to remember how these experiences contributed to your thoughts, body responses, feelings, and actions.

Write these experiences in your journal and discuss them with a family member, friend, or therapist.

You have the tools to move on now.

Once you have learned how to alter your thoughts, body responses, feelings, and actions, you have the tools you will need to move on to a life of healthier relationships.

You cannot change the past, but you can focus on what you can change in yourself and in your relationships *NOW.* You now have new ways of being in the world that are free of shame and guilt.

CHAPTER 6

HEALING SHAME AND GUILT IN YOUR RELATIONSHIPS

Maximizing Healing

Chapter Five presented ways to leave behind old patterns of guilt and shame when dealing with your family of origin. This chapter concerns how to interact with the relationships in the remaining circles in healthy ways that are free of the restrictions of excessive shame and guilt.

Getting close to others carries certain risks. When you let someone else get close to you, they not only learn about all your wonderful qualities. They also learn about your vulnerabilities – all of the things that hurt inside of you, and how to push your emotional buttons.

These close people really get to know your insecurities, including what makes you feel ashamed, and what makes you feel guilty. For that reason, these individuals can really make a difference in your life, for better or worse, you might say. The key to this section on close relationships is how to maximize the healing from shame and guilt that can occur through these relationships.

There is much you can do with a caring and understanding friend or significant other to let go of the tendencies toward shame and guilt you have brought with you into adulthood. A person who is close to you can sometimes point out situations in which you are drowning in guilt or shame, and be the life preserver that saves you.

Relationships: Your Contribution and Their Contribution

Because relationships involve two people, you always have to keep in mind your own behavior and that of the other person. This is an important point, that may seem obvious. Any difficulty in a relationship is always the product of the interactions between both parties, so responsibility never belongs to only one person. Therefore, as you consider your own relationships, it is essential that you learn to recognize your own tendencies towards shame or guilt that you bring to the relationship in terms of your feelings, thoughts and behaviors, as well as those of the other person. Let us first look at how you can learn more about your own contribution to shame and guilt in your relationships.

Your Contribution:
Choosing Healthy Relationships

Choosing relationships well is the first step in reducing shame and guilt arising from these relationships. The best thing you can do to keep yourself from being involved in a relationship that is shaming and blaming you is to never enter such a relationship at all.

However, you may have already found yourself choosing relationships in which you feel shame or guilt. Learning to choose relationships that are free of guilt and shame can be very challenging.

So how do you choose well in relationships? As with many other things related to personal growth, awareness of your own relationship patterns is the first step.

Sometimes it is hard for us to even see shaming and guilt-inducing behaviors in others, because being treated that way may feel so familiar to us. Thus, we may not notice the unhealthy factors that come into play in our choice of relationships.

Awareness of your relationship patterns involves looking at your relationship history, starting with your family of origin. You can use the activities in Chapter Five to help you become aware of the shaming and blaming behaviors that you experienced in your family of origin.

Once you have done this, it is important to consider whether you are choosing adult relationships in which these same shaming and blaming behaviors occur.

Therefore, as you work through the activities in this chapter about identifying shaming and blaming behaviors in your current relationships, keep in mind how these behaviors may be rooted in what you learned in your family of origin.

Your Contribution:
Your Shame and Guilt Buttons

Another important aspect of knowing yourself is to be aware of what your emotional buttons are. Everybody's buttons are different.

What are the buttons or triggers that make you feel shame or guilt? In order to discover this, use the next activity.

ACTIVITY 1: YOUR SHAME BUTTONS

Here is a checklist of common triggers for feelings of shame. Check all that apply to you.

- ☐ Being criticized by someone you respect
- ☐ Making less money than your partner
- ☐ Being the butt of someone's joke
- ☐ Being teased or judged regarding some personal characteristic
- ☐ Being told you disappointed someone
- ☐ Knowing you caused someone else pain, even if unavoidable
- ☐ Being unable to satisfy your partner sexually
- ☐ Feeling like no one else feels the way you do
- ☐ Being unable to do something for yourself
- ☐ Being unable to control your children
- ☐ Being unavailable to your children or partner
- ☐ Spending too much money
- ☐ Eating too much
- ☐ Needing help from others
- ☐ Crying in public
- ☐ Having your abilities underestimated
- ☐ Being seen as incompetent
- ☐ Having someone else be angry at you
- ☐ Having less money than others
- ☐ Being told that others think badly of you

ACTIVITY 2: YOUR GUILT BUTTONS

Here is a checklist of common triggers for feelings of guilt. Check all that apply to you.

☐ Being criticized by someone you respect

☐ Making less money than your partner

☐ Being the butt of someone's joke

☐ Being teased or judged regarding some personal characteristic

☐ Being told you disappointed someone

☐ Knowing you caused someone else pain, even if unavoidable

☐ Being unable to satisfy your partner sexually

☐ Feeling like no one else feels the way you do

☐ Being unable to do something for yourself

☐ Being unable to control your children

☐ Being unavailable to your children or partner

☐ Spending too much money

☐ Eating too much

☐ Needing help from others

☐ Crying in public

☐ Having your abilities underestimated

☐ Being seen as incompetent

☐ Having someone else be angry at you

☐ Having less money than others

☐ Being told that others think badly of you

It is hoped that going through these lists will help you pinpoint the types of experiences that push your shame or guilt buttons. This awareness can then help you to understand when you react or overreact to these types of situations. As mentioned earlier, in every relationship and every interaction, there are two contributing parties. Once you have discovered these areas of vulnerability, you can then work within yourself, using the mind/body/feeling/action model presented in Chapter Four, to decrease your feelings of shame and guilt.

Shame, Guilt and Power in Close Relationships

It does not matter how old or mature we get, we still like to have things our way. We feel safe when we are able to control the things around us – like who we see, what we do, or how others treat us. Unfortunately, we are not very often given the chance to control all of those factors in our lives. Often we are exposed to things which make us feel uncomfortable, sad, scared, or humiliated. The way we learn to avoid these unpleasant experiences is by exercising power.

Having power effectively means that we are able to get our way, and to have control in the relationship. That is, when we do not like something in our environment, somehow we are able to change it.

When you have power in an interpersonal relationship, whether it be a romantic relationship, friendship or relationship within the workplace, it means that the other person listens to your preferences and needs, and those needs are taken into account in decision-making. Negotiation and decision-making involve even the simplest aspects of daily life. The person with power can determine which restaurant is chosen for dinner, which toothpaste will be used, which car will be bought, how children will be raised, or which friends are seen on a regular basis. People in relationships negotiate these issues on a daily basis.

Relationships can either be balanced or unbalanced in terms of power. Some relationships involve just one individual having the majority of the power, whereas other relationships have the two people sharing power. Power is one of the most central issues in all types of relationships. In every relationship, a great deal of energy and many types of behaviors are directed at attaining power.

So what exactly does power have to with shame and guilt? Both shaming and guilt-inducing behaviors can be used to gain power in relationships. When we shame others, we literally humiliate them. A visual image of this situation would be that of a person stepping on top of someone else in order to end up on top. Couples do this endless jockeying for power in many of their arguments. In order to understand the ever-present nature of power contests in relationships, we need to look at our own behaviors and those of others.

When we use guilt to influence or control others, we attack at the level of their conscience, trying to make them feel that they have done something wrong. Usually we feel that this wrong can only be corrected by an apology and/or some way of doing penance. The apology is an acknowledgment that a wrong occurred, and the penance is a way of making up for it. (We're usually more than ready to supply suggestions about what someone could do to make it up to us).

Shame and Domestic Violence

Couples also use shaming to achieve dominance in their relationship. Because shaming behaviors often provoke others, they frequently lead to retaliation. Often this style of conflict can escalate to an explosion and even violence, particularly in couple relationships. Martha and Kyle are a classic example of this type of escalating conflict based on shaming behaviors.

Martha and Kyle had been together for four years when they sought marital therapy for domestic violence. Kyle continually puts Martha down and blames her for everything, which makes her feel ashamed. Martha is an alcoholic who is newly in recovery. Since her recovery began, the conflict between them has intensified, and Martha has begun to get physically out of control. She has punched walls, violently pulled Kyle's hair, and thrown things at him. Martha can no longer tolerate Kyle's continual criticisms, because she no longer has alcohol to help her calm down her angry feelings. They ended up in the emergency room one night when one of the objects she threw hit Kyle in the eye.

Kyle talks about Martha's being out of control with her drinking in the past and her current violent behavior, but does not see himself as playing a part in their conflicts. Martha tends to ignore Kyle unless he is shaming her. He has found that shaming Martha seems to be the most powerful way of getting her attention.

Kyle does not feel very good about himself, and he criticizes Martha as a way of bringing her down a peg and feeling superior. In turn, Martha brings Kyle down a peg by intimidating him through physical violence.

The example of Kyle and Martha illustrates how central shame can be in domestic violence situations. Because both shame and physical violence can be used to achieve dominance, they tend to coincide in relationships.

One can be thought of as verbal abuse (shaming behaviors) and the other as physical abuse (domestic violence).

We can think of shaming others as a way of passing on what has been done to us.

Shame feels so painful that it feels better to externalize it by literally trying to pass it on to someone else. That is why people who were shamed regularly during childhood tend to be the most shaming towards others. People who feel good about themselves and who have no secret pain held in shame inside them don't feel the need to attack others or bring them down a peg.

Shame and Power

Shame can be a devastatingly effective weapon. It is so useful, because it kills two birds with one stone. It makes someone else feel bad, and it can make us feel better. If you feel shameful about yourself, you might want to bring the people around you down a few pegs in order to feel a little better.

The problem with this strategy is that it doesn't really heal your shame. A sense of self-respect cannot be built on a foundation of disrespect for others. In order to become more personally and emotionally aware of how your shaming behaviors impact your relationships, do the activity below.

ACTIVITY 3: YOUR
SHAMING BEHAVIORS

Think back to a time when you shamed someone close to you, and write down the answers
to the questions below.

Was this person a significant other or a friend?

What was the specific behavior you did that
was shaming?

Did you use your knowledge of that person to
decide what would be particularly shaming to
him or her? That is, did you use your knowledge of that person's buttons?

How were you feeling right before the shaming
behavior? (This is important, because we often
retaliate when we ourselves are feeling
ashamed or in a one-down position).

How did the other person react?

Was there anything observable that occurred in the other person that let you know you had hit your mark? i.e., embarrassment, blushing, withdrawal from the room, crying, shouting in retaliation, becoming violent, giving in to you in an argument?

How did you feel after you saw the other person's reaction? Be honest – if you felt victorious glee, admit that. If you felt guilt or remorse for having hurt the other person, describe that.

How did you feel about yourself as a person after the shaming incident?

Guilt and Power

Just as people try to dominate their relationships by shaming others, people can also try to have power in relationships by using guilt.

Guilt is something we try to avoid as much as possible, and avoiding or escaping it will make us do all kinds of things we would otherwise not want to do.

If someone can make us feel guilt with their words or actions, we suddenly become more pliable, more easily manipulated to do what others want from us.

As with shaming behaviors, a good way to get in touch with blaming (guilt-producing) behaviors and how they affect your relationships is to look first at your own guilt-producing behaviors towards others.

In order to become more personally and emotionally aware of how your guilt-producing behaviors impact your relationships, do the next activity.

ACTIVITY 4: YOUR GUILT-PRODUCING BEHAVIORS TOWARDS OTHERS

Think back to a time when you tried to provoke guilt in a friend or significant other, and write down the answers to the questions below.

Was this person a significant other or a friend?

What was the specific behavior you did that was guilt-producing?

Did you use your knowledge of that person's vulnerabilities to decide what would make that person feel guilty? That is, did you use your knowledge of that person's guilt buttons?

How were you feeling right before the guilt-producing behavior?

How did the other person react?

Was there anything observable that occurred in the other person that let you know you'd hit your mark? i.e., defensiveness, asking for forgiveness, apologizing, attempting to make you feel guilty in retaliation, giving in to you in an argument?

How did you feel after you saw the other person's reaction? Be honest – if you felt victorious glee, admit that. If you felt bad for having manipulated the other person, describe that. How did you feel about yourself as a person after this incident?

Their Contribution: Looking at How Others Bring Shame and Guilt into the Relationship

Now that we have looked at your contribution to shame and guilt in your relationships, it is time to consider what the other party of the relationship brings into the situation. The clearest way to think of the contribution of others is to consider their shaming and blaming behaviors.

Often we are not aware of the things that others do which lead us to feel ashamed or guilty. Once we are able to identify what those behaviors are, we are many steps closer to reducing their power over us.

If you feel feelings of shame or guilt every time you are around a certain person, that is an important sign that perhaps unhealthy shaming or blaming behaviors are occurring.

Shame Contributed by Others

Sometimes it may be very difficult for you to identify exactly what shaming behaviors are occurring. In order to help you do this identification process, focus first on shame feelings, and use the next activity.

ACTIVITY 5: A TIME WHEN SOMEONE SHAMED YOU

Think back to a time when someone shamed you, and write down answers to these questions.

. Was this person a significant other or a friend?

What was the specific behavior this person did that was shaming?

Did this person use their knowledge of your vulnerabilities to decide how to best shame you? That is, did the person use their knowledge of your buttons?

Was this person reacting to anything that you were aware of? For example, was this person retaliating because you had just shamed him or her, or were they taking something out on you because they were feeling small or powerless?

How did you react? i.e., embarrassment, blushing, withdrawal from the room, crying, shouting in retaliation, becoming violent, giving in to them in an argument?

How did you feel about yourself as a person after the shaming incident?

Guilt Contributed by Others

Jack has noticed that he frequently feels guilty around his wife. He would sometimes rather not be around her. She says that he has not been doing enough around the house to help out. Jack has asked her what she would like for him to do, and she usually says, "Oh, don't worry about it. It's all done." When Jack says that he's sorry, she says, "I forgive you. I'm used to it."

What do you see in this example that would create guilt in Jack? What do you suppose Jack thinks when he hears this from his wife? Exactly what is it that his wife is saying that would create guilt? After all, she says that she forgives him. Does that make her seem like a forgiving, kind person? Or is there another message embedded in her words that says that she does not really forgive him at all?

Jack's wife is giving a mixed message. She is expressing distress and anger, thus passing along her distress to Jack, but she's blocking any attempts he makes to fix the situation. He is forced to sit with his guilt, and just endure it. There is nothing he can do to change it. Or is there? As stated before, the first step is awareness of what his wife's guilt-producing behaviors are.

In order to explore this issue in your own relationships, use the next activity.

ACTIVITY 6: A TIME WHEN SOMEONE TRIED TO PROVOKE GUILT IN YOU

Think back to a time when someone attempted to provoke guilt in you, and write down answers to these questions.

Was this person a significant other or a friend?

What was the specific behavior this person did that was guilt-producing?

Did this person use their knowledge of your vulnerabilities to decide how to best create guilt in you? That is, did the person use their knowledge of your guilt "buttons?"

Was this person reacting to anything that you were aware of? That is, what was the motive for trying to make you feel guilty? For example, was this person retaliating because you had just tried to make him or her feel guilty?

Was this person trying to jockey for power in your relationship by making you feel indebted to him or her?

How did you react? i.e., Did you try to defend yourself by justifying your actions? Did you become physically violent? Did you give in to this person in an argument?

How did you feel about yourself as a person after the incident?

Do you think the guilt-producing person got what they wanted from the incident? That is, did they get the outcome they desired?

It is hoped that through these activities involving looking at your own shaming and guilt-producing actions
as well as those of others, that you have gained an
understanding of how guilt and shame are used in relationships to establish power.

We can all use our knowledge of each others' vulnerabilities to influence or even control others. We all learn
what each others' shame and guilt buttons are, and we
are tempted to use them against each other when the
going gets tough. However, the problem with this
approach is that in so doing we allow the unhealthy
influences of shame and guilt into the most intimate
parts of our relationships with others. Once we try to
dominate others through shame or guilt, we are also
vulnerable to being dominated. A relationship in which
two people fight continually for dominance or power
cannot be fertile soil to grow some of the things we
want from our relationships.

Healthy relationships can transform our lives and our
selves by giving us acceptance, companionship, understanding, compassion, and love. When you consider an
atmosphere of fear and competition for power, and of
using others' vulnerabilities against them, how can that
atmosphere support those positive things that relationships
can provide? When we use shaming and guilt-producing
behaviors to influence others, or when we tolerate those
behaviors to be used on us, we allow weeds to choke out
the best that can come from our relationships.

The Solution: A Commitment to Equality of Power in Relationships

So what is the solution? How can we invest the best we have in our relationships, and keep out the weeds of shame and guilt? If guilt and shaming behaviors help people to come out "on top" in relationships, the solution is to try to equalize power in your relationships. What does this equality mean, and how can you attain it?

Step 1

The first step is to make a commitment to yourself that you will not engage in shaming or guilt-producing behaviors with others. It will take a lot of self-awareness on your part to keep this commitment, because old habits are very hard to break.

An example of a commitment to respectful behavior towards others.

In order to examine this commitment further, let's look at what happened with Lena, who made this commitment to non-shaming, non-blaming behaviors in her life. Lena has been close friends with Rosa since they were both in high school, and they began renting an apartment together a year ago.

Since getting the apartment, a number of household issues have surfaced which have created conflict between them. Lena notices that Rosa never seems to want to do her share of the housework, and she has developed a habit of trying to make Rosa feel guilty.

So what would happen if Lena made a commitment towards being respectful to her roommate rather than provoking guilt or shame? Does that mean that she has to just accept Rosa as she is? Not at all. Lena should not simply accept her roommate's lack of attention to household chores. It does need to be addressed, but Lena needs to learn to talk to her roommate about this problem in a new way. Here are three examples of ways in which Lena could communicate with her roommate.

Communicating in a "guilt-producing" way:

"I do everything around here every single day. You haven't lifted a finger since we moved here, and now I've developed a back ache from all the cleaning I've had to do on my own." This statement asserts that the roommate's inaction on the cleaning front has actually caused Lena to suffer physically. Although it may be true that Lena has developed a back ache from all the cleaning, communicating in this way is likely to provoke her roommate into being defensive, because it lays the guilt on so thick.

Communicating in a shaming way:

"You are so lazy – you've probably never lifted a finger in your life to help anyone when it comes to housework." Why is this message shaming? Because it not only criticizes her roommate's behavior, but her being as well, by telling her she's lazy (a personal characteristic).

In addition, this statement attacks her roommate's past behavior and makes unfounded assumptions about that as well.

Communicating in a respectful way:

"I've noticed that I do the majority of the chores around here. Would you be willing to follow through on your chores without being reminded? Otherwise, I think we're going to have a problem living together, and I don't want it to affect our friendship. Let's try to work on this." What is respectful about this way of communicating? It is not demanding, and it does not attack the other person in any way. The statement is an observation ("I've noticed"), and it also treats the other person as an adult.

The person who is confronted in this respectful way is more likely to be motivated to work on things rather than spending energy defending himself or herself.

Step 2

Do not tolerate shaming and blaming behaviors from others in your relationships. Now we are considering the situation from the perspective of being on the receiving end of shaming or blaming behaviors from others. When you feel that someone is trying to control you through shame or guilt-producing actions or words, do not accept it.

It is important for you to develop a strategy to keep yourself from being harmed by the other person's actions. There are many strategies you can use to not accept shaming and blaming behaviors from others, and you can choose whatever option best suits you and the situation at hand.

In order to think about how to keep from being shamed or blamed by others, let us consider the two sides of the roommate situation between Lena and Rosa.

Rosa says this about the situation: "I know that I don't really do much cleaning in the apartment, but I do a lot of cooking, and Lena always eats my food! So I feel like it sort of equals out. She probably doesn't think so, but she's really nit picky about the cleaning stuff. I didn't realize that we were so opposite until after we'd already moved in together. I also didn't know she could be such a nag. It really gets on my nerves and I start to feel bad – it's like living with my mother, which is what I was trying to get away from."

Fortunately for Rosa, she has a number of options of what she could do to try to resolve this problem with Lena. These options roughly fall into three categories, and can be applied in nearly any situation in which someone is being shamed or blamed.

Option 1: Use the direct (verbal) approach.

Communicate respectfully and assertively how you feel when someone else directs shaming or blaming behaviors at you.

For example, perhaps Rosa could say, "You know, Lena, when you say that I've probably never cleaned anything in my life and you call me lazy, it makes me feel really terrible about myself, like I'm a four-year-old or something. Not only that, it feels like a personal attack. I don't mind you giving me feedback, but could you try to make it a little less harsh?"

This approach lets Lena know how her feedback feels on the receiving end, and it does not counter attack. Imagine for a moment how Lena would be likely to react if Rosa were to gently confront her in this way.

In contrast, Rosa could use an absolutely unproductive approach by attacking back. She could say something like, "Oh yeah? Well I don't see you lifting a finger anywhere near the kitchen, and I don't hear you complaining about all the food I cook that you eat and eat and eat."

Now imagine how Lena would be likely to react if Rosa confronted her in this attacking way, and imagine how different it would be than her response to a more respectful approach.

Option 2: Take responsibility.

Sometimes other people get their ammunition for their shaming and blaming from our irresponsible behavior. For example, if your significant other has to nearly harass you to get you to follow through on your agreement to take out the trash, you're sort of asking for shaming and blaming behaviors from your significant other. Although your behavior does not justify others in shaming or blaming you, it is more likely that others will stop shaming and blaming you if they see you doing your part in meeting your obligations.

Option 3: Change your response.

You cannot always make someone stop their shaming and blaming behavior, but you can change your response to it. This option works especially well when the direct verbal approach has failed.

For example, suppose Rosa already talked to Lena

about Lena's nagging, shaming behaviors, and Lena continues to nag anyway. Rosa could decide that each time the nagging begins, she will leave the room rather than sit and listen to it.

The "change your response" approach gives the message that nagging, shaming behavior will not be listened to and is not acceptable.

Another situation in which changing your response would be appropriate would be with someone who does not respond to verbal confrontation of any kind. We all know people who refuse to accept feedback or take responsibility for their own behavior. A verbal confrontation with this type of person can be useless or can even make a bad situation worse.

Instead of wasting time with a verbal confrontation about this type of person's shaming or blaming behaviors, it would be best to change one's actions in such a way that make the shaming or blaming behaviors less likely to occur.

Here is an example of a creative response one man used to deal with his boss' shaming statements.

Rick was a contractor who did a wide range of repair work. He was new to this kind of work, and was being apprenticed by his boss, Don, a crusty old guy who had burned out on contracting work and probably should have retired about five years back.

There were other people working under Don as well, because it was a big contracting company. Don had a pretty harsh way of talking to his employees, especially when they were new, and a lot of people quit before finishing their training with him.

After working for Don for a few months, Rick said the following: "The tough thing about being trained by Don was that he wasn't consistent. Some days he'd say to do things one way, and the next day he'd say another way. The only thing you could rely on with Don was criticism. He seemed to want to bring you down a peg. No matter what you said about your work, he'd argue with you about it. If you said black, he'd say white. There was only one guy on the crew that Don never messed with like that. So I started watching this guy, and I noticed that he never argued with Don. In fact, he'd ask Don for feedback, while the rest of us avoided Don like he was the plague. So one day I tried that, just as a little game to see if it would get him off my back. I even exaggerated it a little, saying that I could really use a little feedback because I didn't think I'd done a very good job on something. Don started arguing with me again, true to form, but this time, he was telling me that I should stop criticizing my work like that, that I was doing a great job. I could not believe my ears. I laughed all the way home that day, because I finally felt like I'd won the game. Never had a problem with Don after that."

This example illustrates how sometimes a change in your response behavior can break someone else's pattern of shaming or blaming. If you change your behavior, you can throw the other person off guard, and something new can happen between you.

Option 4: Reinvest your energy.

Many of us spend endless amounts of energy trying to get other people to change, and it just does not work. It is important to remember that we have choices when someone else's shaming or blaming behaviors begin to wear down our strength and self-respect.

Life is short, and we have a limited amount of energy to invest during our lifetimes. It is better to invest that energy in more positive pursuits with a better return for our energy than to stay in a chronically unhealthy interpersonal situation.

Reinvesting your energy can have many meanings. For some people, reinvesting energy will involve actually leaving the situation. For others, the solution might just be a shift in thinking, such as realizing that the boss' opinion of them might not be all that important after all.

Finding support and self-respect in other areas is always helpful in making yourself less vulnerable to others' shaming or blaming behaviors.

Take, for instance, the waiter who puts up with a lot of disrespect from customers because he is more strongly invested in his talent for doing art outside of work. His customers' disrespect rolls off his back, because he just is not invested in what they think.

Another way of reinvesting energy can be to lower your expectations of people who shame or blame you, and then limit your contact with them. By lowering your expectations of them, you force yourself to become more realistic about them ever changing.

If you stop trying to change them, you free up your energy to seek support from people who are capable of loving you as you are. Reinvest your energy in developing a supportive network of friends or family with whom you can just be accepted as yourself.

Options one through four give you many tools to use in order to stop tolerating shaming and blaming behaviors in your relationships.

Using these tools, you can work towards equalizing power in all of your relationships. In order to begin this process, do the next activity.

ACTIVITY 7: PUTTING THE OPTIONS INTO PRACTICE

Think about a personal situation in which someone in your life tries to influence you through shaming or blaming behaviors. Using the three options listed above, brainstorm how you could get this person to stop these behaviors.

Option 1: The direct (verbal) approach. Write down what you could say to this person to communicate in a respectful but assertive way that these behaviors need to stop. What do you think this person's response would be to your verbal confrontation?

Option 2: Take responsibility. Is there anything that you could do that would stop "fueling" the shaming and blaming behaviors of this person? For example, is there any truth to their feedback, even if the way they give it to you is not respectful? How do you think this person would react if you became more responsible in this area? If there are things you could change, make a plan of how you will do it.

Option 3: Change your response. Take a moment to brainstorm different responses you could make to the disrespectful behavior of this person. Can you think of anything that would make it more difficult for that person to shame or blame you? Can you imagine anything you could do that would break or disrupt this person's negative shaming or blaming pattern? Be creative.

Option 4: Reinvest your energy. Think about
your priorities in life. Take some time right now
to write out in a lifelong sense, the 5-10 most
important things in your life. Now make a list
of the five top problems that have most
annoyed, worried or otherwise disturbed you in
the past month.

How do these problems fit in with your lifelong priorities? Are there any shifts you would like to make in order to have your energy investment more closely match what is really most important to you? If so, write them down now.

Now think about how you might feel at the end of your life. Will you feel satisfied with the ways you chose to invest your precious life energy on a daily basis? Consider whether you'd make any changes in energy investment.

Make a plan of how you will incorporate these changes into your daily life, starting now.

By making these shifts in priorities, the shaming and blaming people in our lives lose their power over us. We become empowered to choose the very best for ourselves.

The Solution: Taking Action Against Shame and Guilt in Your General Environment

Your general environment consists of your acquaintances, strangers, and even societal influences that can create guilt or shame in you. Even influences like these to which you are not exposed daily can impact you. Fortunately, most of the activities about daily interpersonal situations presented earlier in the chapter can be applied even at the level of acquaintances and strangers should they act in shaming or guilt-provoking ways towards you.

For example, if a stranger does something rude or disrespectful towards you, you have several options from which to choose your response. Depending on the particulars of the incident, you can choose the response which will be the safest, most self-respecting and other-respecting option.

In addition to the options you might need for problems in relationships with others, sometimes you might encounter a disrespectful situation that is not interpersonal in nature.

Consider Jared's experience as an example. He is an African-American attorney who joined a law firm eight years ago, where he is the only non-white attorney.

 Since joining the firm he has won some of the high profile cases the firm has taken. For the past two years, he has begun to wonder if he will ever be asked to be a partner in the firm. He suspects that he was hired as a token to improve the image of the firm, but that he cannot expect to advance as far as his white colleagues.

He recently saw a white colleague who is also a close friend become a partner after being there less time than himself. He hesitates to bring this up to the partners, because he does not want to be labeled as a troublemaker.

However, every time he sees his friend, he feels angry.

When he squelches those angry feelings, then he feels ashamed for not sticking up for himself.

The dilemma in which Jared finds himself is not uncommon. He is stuck with two unattractive choices: to act or go on accepting the situation.

Rather than being an interpersonal issue, what Jared faces is discrimination that may end up in a legal battle. His workplace is undervaluing him, and it makes him feel ashamed to put up with that. What should he do to help himself in this shaming work environment?

Shame that comes from the general environment, such as in Jared's case, is difficult to tackle. It was easy for others to discount his experience, and it was hard to prove exactly what the source of the problem was. For example, his law firm could easily argue that Jared's lack of advancement had nothing to do with his ethnic background.

In the beginning, Jared had even questioned himself about whether discrimination was really happening, and tried to convince himself not to be upset.

Jared sought support from his brother, who had also experienced subtle and not-so-subtle devaluing actions from employers because of their discomfort with an African American in a professional role. Getting this support helped Jared to stop shaming himself, and to hold his law firm accountable for their actions.

Rather than accepting the situation, he decided to raise the issue with the partners, and even take legal action if necessary. What Jared found once he decided to take action was that his shame feelings disappeared, and his self-respect grew.

Probably the least personal but very powerful influence we experience in our general environment is the media, and it can contain messages that provoke feelings of shame or guilt in us. Often messages containing negative stereotypes can make us feel powerless and ashamed of who we are. We are not usually aware of how much those messages can shape what we believe about ourselves.

For example, the women we often see on television always seem to trip while being chased by an attacker and must be rescued by some heroic male figure.

How can a woman develop a positive sense of strength with this kind of message? Because of overexposure to these portrayals of women, many women develop a sense of shame, believing themselves to be weak and helpless.

Any group of people who is consistently portrayed in a negative light in the media will find it hard to have a proud sense of their own identity, free of shame.

Activism against Shame and Guilt in the Media

What can you do to heal from shame or guilt which comes from such an impersonal source as the media?

As was stated in an earlier part of this chapter, the key is: Do not tolerate shaming or blaming messages. Make a commitment to yourself that you will only support media that portray people without negative stereotypes. Use your judgment when you see certain media offerings advertised, and do not choose to watch, listen to, or read things which humiliate people.

You may even choose to become more active by writing, calling or e-mailing the media when you become aware of objectionable material.

Some people find that the most healing thing they can do for themselves is to reject shaming or blaming messages by actively protesting them in this way.

REFERENCES

REFERENCES

Ausubel, D. 1955. *Relationships between guilt and shame in the socializing process.* Psychological Review, 62: 378- 390.

Borysenko, J. 1990. *Guilt is the Teacher, Love is the Lesson.* New York, New York: Warner Books, Inc.

Bradshaw, J. 1988. *Healing the Shame That Binds You.* Deerfield Beach, Florida: Health Communications, Inc.

Broucek, F. 1991. *Shame and the Self.* New York: The Guilford Press.

Catalano, E.M. 1987. *The Chronic Pain Control Workbook.* Oakland, CA: New Harbinger Publications, Inc.

Davis, M., Eshelman, E., McKay, M. 1988. *The Relaxation and Stress Reduction Workbook.* Oakland, CA: New Harbinger Publications, Inc.

English, F. 1975. *Shame and Social Control.* Transactional Analysis Journal, 5: 24- 28.

Fischer, B. 1988. "The Process of Healing Shame." In *The Treatment of Shame and Guilt in Alcoholism Counseling,* edited by Potter- Efron, R., and Potter-Efron, P. New York: Haworth Press.

Flanigan, B. 1988. "Shame and Forgiving in Alcoholism." In *The Treatment of Shame and Guilt in Alcoholism Counseling,* edited by Potter- Efron, R., and Potter-Efron, P. New York: Haworth Press.

Fossum, M., and Mason, M. 1986. *Facing Shame.* New York, New York: W. W. Norton & Co.

Jacoby, M. 1994. *Shame and the Origins of Self-esteem: A Jungian Approach.* London: Routledge.

Kaufman, G. 1996. *The Psychology of Shame.* New York, New York: Springer Publishing Co.

Kaufman, G., and Bly, R. 1995. "Healing internalized shame." In *Men Healing Shame,* by Schenk., R., and Everingham, J. New York: Springer.

Kaufman, G. 1985. *Shame: The Power of Caring.* 2d ed. Cambridge, Mass.: Schenkman Books, Inc.

Kornfield, J. 1993. *A Path with Heart: A Guide Through the Perils and Promises of Spiritual Life.* New York, NY: Bantam Books

Lansky, M. 1987. "Shame and Domestic Violence." In *The Many Faces of Shame,* edited by Nathanson, D. New York: Guilford Press.

Lewis, H. 1971. *Shame and Guilt in Neurosis.* New York: International Universities Press, Inc.

Middelton- Moz, J. 1990. *Shame and Guilt: The Masters of Disguise.* Deerfield, Florida: Health Communications, Inc.

Nathanson, D. 1987. "A Timetable For Shame." In *The Many Faces of Shame,* edited by Nathanson, D. New York: Guilford Press.

Piers, G., and Singer, M. 1953. *Shame and Guilt.* Springfield, ILL.: Charles Thomas.

Potter- Efron, R., and Potter- Efron, P. 1989. *Letting Go of Shame: Understanding How Shame Affects Your Life.* Center City, MN: Hazelden.

Potter- Efron, R., and Potter- Efron, P. 1988. *The Treatment of Shame and Guilt in Alcoholism* Counseling. Binghamton, New York: The Haworth Press, Inc.

Salzberg, S. 1995. *Lovingkindness: The Revolutionary Art of Happiness.* Boston, MA: Shambhala Publications, Inc.

Schneider, C. 1987. " A Mature Sense of Shame." In *The Many Faces of Shame*, edited by Nathanson, D. New York: Guilford Press.

Schneider, C. 1987. "A Mature Sense of Shame." In *The Many Faces of Shame,* edited by Nathanson, D. New York: Guilford Press.

Smith, M. 1975. *When I Say No I Feel Guilty.* New York, New York: Bantam Books.

Tomkins, S. 1987. "Shame." *In The Many Faces of Shame,* edited by Nathanson, D. New York: Guilford Press.